HOW TO SELL YOUR IDEA TO HOLLYWOOD

HOW TO SELL YOUR IDEA TO HOLLYWOOD

Robert Kosberg

WITH MIM EICHLER

HarperPerennial
A Division of HarperCollins*Publishers*

FIRST EDITION

Designed by Helene Berinsky

Library of Congress Cataloging-in-Publication Data

Kosberg, Robert.
    How to sell your idea to Hollywood / by Robert Kosberg with Mim Eichler.
—1st HarperPerennial ed.
      p. cm.
    ISBN 0-06-096569-X (pbk.)
    1. Motion picture authorship. 2. Motion picture industry—United States
—Vocational guidance. I. Eichler, Mim. II. Title.
PN1996.K66 1991   90-55976
808.2'3—dc20

---

93   94   95   96   97   RRD   10   9   8   7   6   5   4   3   2

For Susan, Michael, and Ruth

"In the dizzying world of moviemaking, we must not be distracted from one fundamental concept: The idea is king.

Stars, directors, writers, hardware, special effects, new sound systems . . . all of these can have a role to play in the success of a film, but they all must serve as humble subjects to the supremacy of the idea."

—Jeffrey Katzenberg

CONTENTS

ACKNOWLEDGMENTS

The authors wish to thank literary agent Sherry Robb for helping us to create this project and for guiding us along the way.

For their humor, help, and insights, we are deeply grateful to senior editor Craig Nelson and assistant editor Jennifer Hull at HarperCollins.

Thanks also to Rosemary Sneeringer for her research and writing talents early on.

Sincere appreciation is due to Jeanine Gruber, administrative assistant to Robert Kosberg, for her expediency and enthusiasm.

A hearty thank-you goes out to every individual whose experience in the process of selling to Hollywood is mentioned in this book. While we are unable to acknowledge all of them here, our appreciation goes out to the Writers Guild West and to Rick Pamplin and Chris Vogler for lending us their time and expertise. We wish to applaud everyone named in this book for their efforts in the industry and to thank them for allowing us to share their stories with our readers.

Special thanks to Ruth, Susan, and Michael.

AUTHORS' NOTE

In presenting a book about how ideas work in Hollywood, we have provided information that is mainly based on our observations and experience. We have, to the best of our abilities, attempted to confirm dates, figures, titles, names, and spellings. To any of those who failed to gain mention in conjunction with the various projects described, or who were not available for verification of the spelling of their names, the authors make all due apologies.

INTRODUCTION

The book you are about to read contains information which I certainly wish I'd known when I was first starting out in Hollywood. I had grown up loving the movies, eagerly looking forward to all of them—the comedies, the thrillers, the adventure/action pictures, the fantasies and the horror flicks, the romances, the classics, even foreign films and so-called art movies. And I always knew instinctively that I wanted nothing more than just to be a part of the moviemaking process. So when, as a young adult, I set my sights on being a screenwriter and worked diligently to master my craft, it was a bit discouraging when I encountered the many obstacles that are thrown in the path of the Hollywood neophyte. In time, however, the tables have turned. Through trial and error, with a little luck and a bit of ingenuity, I was able to come up with a system to beat "the system."

In brief, my approach began as a way of testing out material before sitting down and writing a whole screenplay. Before long, I discovered that the marketing test itself could quickly translate into a sale. Material can get you into Hollywood in a variety of ways, regardless of whether you are a writer, an aspiring director or producer, or someone with ideas. This book differs from the various screenwriting manuals you may have read in that it focuses on the very heart of the script: the idea. What we will see as we move on is what power an idea can have in Hollywood. An idea can give you access to the film industry and present a wide array of financial and professional opportunities. Or shall we say in words more suited to the glamour of the movies: A mere idea can bring you fame and fortune (or at the very least a job).

It is with great pleasure that I am able to present a book about the wonderful potential of ideas, as a way of encouraging people at all levels who are attempting to get their break in the business. For those of you writers and producers already on the "inside" (or you who have had some experience), you may want to use the guidelines in this book as a way to revitalize and refresh your career, as a reminder of your own potential to come up with the next blockbuster movie idea. For another group of you who are just now contemplating taking a stab at Hollywood, it is my hope that the principles of finding and selling ideas will speed you more easily and securely toward your goals. And last but not least, for those of you everywhere and anywhere who never thought that you had something to offer to the movies, I hope this book helps you to realize that just maybe you do.

I have yet to meet a person who didn't have at least one idea for a movie. The different kinds of people who attend my seminars are not just film students, but housewives and bartenders and accountants and lawyers. This book will show you how these people have created ideas and learned to sell them. In fact, some of these ideas have made it all the way to your neighborhood theaters.

One of the best parts for me about writing this book is that I have a chance to promote the importance of ideas . . . and, of course, the people who create them. Many people forget about the idea that started everything rolling in the first place. This book will hopefully remind them that without the initial ideas there would be no movies.

I have always been, and always will be, enchanted and inspired by films. In watching the work of those I admire, I used to wonder what it would be like to see one of my own original ideas actually end up on a movie screen. And if any of you have ever dreamt such a dream, or if ever in the future you may stumble onto such an ambition, I can tell you what an overwhelmingly gratifying feeling it is when it happens. And it can happen for you.

With all the many ideas that I have sold—the projects that I have written and/or produced, the TV movies and the feature films that have been made from my ideas—one experience that perhaps stands out as the most fulfilling wasn't even in a sale or in the making of one of my movie ideas. Having hatched an idea for a project called "A Novel Life," I found myself engaged in story meetings with one of the world's foremost living playwrights, Tom Stoppard. And although, for various reasons, he didn't go on to write the script, his comment to me about the story was the ultimate compliment I could have ever received. I could have truly died and gone to heaven when Tom Stoppard said to me, "This is a wonderful idea. I wish I had thought of it myself."

Let me say that I hope each and every one of you has the opportunity to hear such words. I hope, too, this book will have helped you get that chance.

CHAPTER 1
HOLLYWOOD, USA

"In a few more years America's self-righteous preachers
would be maligning the movie colony and all its works;
Hollywood, California, became a synonym of Sin. Professional do-gooders would brand Hollywood a New Babylon
whose evil influence rivaled the legendary depravity of the
old; banner headlines and holier-than-thou editorials
would equate Sex, Dope and Movie Stars. Yet while the
country's organized cranks screamed for blood and boy-
cott, the public, unfazed, flocked to the movies in ever-
increasing multitudes."

—On the early days of Hollywood, from
Hollywood Babylon by Kenneth Anger

You've no doubt heard the clichés. While you may have
updated your view from the one above, you may, like many
people, conceive of the back streets of Hollywood as back-
stabbing, ruthless, coldhearted, and cutthroat. Some of you
may even look at the moviemaking world as an exploitive
system that chews up talent and spits it out in little pieces.
(Okay, this part is basically true.) Or perhaps you might
believe the myths about lazy executives who do nothing
more than spout expressions like "Take a meeting" or "Let's
do lunch" or "We'll send it up the flagpole and see if it flies."

Well, I for one try my best not to say, "Take a meeting."
I've never "done" lunch and I've yet to meet a lazy executive
attempting to mount an idea for a project on a flagpole. Con-

1

trary to popular belief, the power brokers in Hollywood are anything but lazy. In fact, my experience with the men and women who successfully wield control in the film industry is that they are dynamic, hardworking, and very bright individuals who share a common cause—the desire to make movies.

The most practical way to understand Hollywood is to view it as a game. Of course, you have to know how to play, if you're going to have any success at all. But perhaps the most important rule is to make sure you love the game. And at whatever stage you are, the ace up your sleeve isn't really youth, as commonly thought, but that quality often associated with youth: *passion*. So remember, to win in Hollywood it doesn't matter who you are or where you are as long as you have that passion.

I have to admit that I wasn't always so optimistic. There was actually a time when I viewed the collective entity known as Hollywood as a big bad wolf. Fresh out of UCLA Film School and having written a few screenplays, I immediately discovered that talent alone didn't pay the rent. Nor did the fact that I'd been able to get an agent ensure my prospects of making a living (although meeting agents who smoke cigars was always fun). But I'm thankful that, with survival being the mother of invention, I soon found myself in a series of "gofer" and assistant jobs that did provide me with opportunities to learn the ground rules of the game I so badly wanted to play. What seemed like a detour on the path I was pursuing led me directly to lesson number one:

DO YOUR HOLLYWOOD HOMEWORK

Without a working knowledge of the "who's who" and the "what's where" in Hollywood, you'll find yourself at a serious disadvantage. Although I do believe that there is no substitute for genuine talent in this business, it's highly important to understand that it *is* a business. Big business. Every time a movie gets made, millions of dollars are at stake. Careers and future livelihoods are being put on the line each and every day. So with that kind of inherent risk, before you can dare hope to have others invest in your vision, make it your business to know as much as you can about the industry.

I stress the importance of doing your homework for several reasons, some of which we'll explore in more depth later. At this stage, the most obvious purpose is to point out the pitfalls that often deter eager beginners. It's obviously not wise to be either overly confident or unduly intimidated. The solution is to take the simple, pragmatic approach. By learning as much as you can about how the Hollywood system works, you can develop a personal strategy that works for you and your goals.

For now, your first fact-finding mission should focus on gathering background on the basic structure of Hollywood. In essence, I'm talking about the hierarchy of the players. Simply described, this entire bustling metropolis, the hundreds of thousands of people employed in film and television, can be separated into two categories—the buyers and the sellers. Understanding the distinction moves us on to lesson number two:

DEVELOP A MARKET MENTALITY

It's true for most people who establish a permanent foothold in Hollywood that they'll alternate buying and selling hats periodically during their careers; sometimes they'll switch roles on a daily basis. I'm definitely an example of someone who has spent equal time on both sides of the desk. But despite the continual flux of names and faces, there is usually an inner circle of people who have most of the power. These are the people who get movies made.

No matter where you currently fit into the Hollywood picture and no matter what your goals may be, it's still very important to know who the real buyers are. After all, you are the one who has something to sell. What you have to sell, by the way, is the very thing Hollywood must have for it to thrive. Like the ground below any huge superstructure, the foundation of this expansive business is composed of properties. And properties are merely scripts or stories based on what you've got to sell—ideas.

I'm by no means suggesting you pitch a tent on Sunset Boulevard with an IDEAS FOR SALE sign posted and expect the studio executives to line up in droves. I'm also not implying that good ideas in themselves will guarantee overnight success; nor that being a razzle-dazzle salesperson will compensate for a mediocre or poorly developed idea. What I do urge is for you to realize that, as in almost any business context, Hollywood functions according to the rules of supply and demand.

Assuming that you have decided to jump into the fray, or that maybe you've already entered into the Hollywood arena, I merely stress developing a solid market mentality. By realizing the simple notion that your ideas are valuable wares to be traded on the open Hollywood market, you can buffer yourself against the initial rejections that occur so frequently. Taking the philosophy that one of your ideas has the potential to one day fill a studio need might help you deal with this next rule of the game:

ACCEPT THE GAMBLE

Like it or not, the odds of scoring a big overnight win in Hollywood aren't any better than hitting the jackpot in a gambling casino, or winning the state lottery. Of course, people do hit jackpots and they also win lotteries. And yes, every now and then, a true story surfaces about the long shot in Hollywood—the struggling waitress in Malibu who writes a screenplay and sells it on her first submission for three hundred thousand dollars. The sad fact is that although it can happen, it is very much an exception to the rule. On the very same week that a story like this shows up in the newspapers, some fifteen thousand hopefuls will start their screenplays. What they don't realize is how staggeringly fortunate that Malibu waitress was. She got lucky.

When you go to Las Vegas, or when you buy your one-dollar lottery ticket, you're accepting the gamble. You hope you'll be lucky, but you know what the odds are. Likewise, when you invest your time, energy, and talent in Hollywood, you have to accept the gamble. There are no money-back guarantees, no bank-insured or low-risk ways to play the game. As in other forms of gambling, there are even unscrupulous types waiting to take advantage.

But there are logical ways to safeguard against such exploitative practices which we'll carefully detail later on. By watching your back at all times and by devising coherent tactics, you can learn to hedge your bets and improve your odds. In time, you will no doubt come to realize that the following cliché is true:

HOLLYWOOD IS A VERY SMALL TOWN

In those first couple of years when I started out, I was doing anything and everything to learn the ropes. I was a driver for a public relations firm, a script reader for Ann-Margret's production company, an agent's assistant at International Creative Management. And I worked in New York reading scripts for the Italian film director Lina Wertmuller.

While working at all of these jobs, I made a simple discovery. I realized that though there were thousands of people in the entertainment industry, only a small fraction of them were responsible for getting a movie made.

Then I began to see how this concentration of real power simply offered the inventive newcomer some terrific time-saving information. Let's take a look at the numbers in sort of a reverse pecking order (for our purposes) and see how this works.

Production Support

Every time you watch the credits roll at the end of a film, you will see anywhere from a couple hundred to several hundred names of various crew personnel who have together played a part in bringing the movie to the screen. Multiply that number by the two hundred or so movies made every year and you can sense the size of the production support population. Also in Hollywood you'll find double that many people working in television production. In addition, there are usually hundreds more vying for each one of those jobs. This should give you an idea of how much competition there is on every level. But the good news is that most of the people who work in production support capacities don't affect you. They will usually not be instrumental in getting your project made. Before we get to the heavyweights who do get movies made, we still have many more heads to count.

Actors

Combined, the actors' unions (Screen Actors Guild, Screen Extras Guild and the American Federation of Television and Radio Artists) report approximately 113,000 members in good standing, which does not account for the many multiples of those numbers trying to break in. It then becomes all the more mind-boggling to realize that only a sheer handful of actors have the clout to get a film made. These are names that will be important to know, as well as how you might get one of your ideas to them, which we'll address further on when we discuss the elements of packaging. In the meantime, I do want to point out that the stars who can get green lights on projects almost always get them from the studios.

Directors

Out of the nine thousand directors currently registered as members of the Directors Guild of America, there are also some with studio deals—or independent production company backing—whose desire to do a film will determine whether it goes or not. The percentage of the total number of directors who receive such carte blanche is very small.

Screenwriters

The Writers Guild, East and West combined, reports approximately 10,300 members. Add to this number anywhere from twenty-five thousand to fifty thousand (the amount of screenplays registered annually by guild and nonguild members plus an estimate of those who've written unregistered scripts) and understand that this represents your competition if you are a writer. Among these numbers there are again a bare minimum who can actually write their own ticket in Hollywood. While the power to get a movie made is seldom associated with the screenwriter, I do advise developing a familiarity with writers who have solid track records or deals with studios. The reason for this will become more apparent as we continue.

Agents, Managers, and Lawyers

As we move ahead, I'll be discussing whether or not you need representation to achieve your goals. For now, all you need to know is that out of the hundreds of franchised and nonfranchised agencies and out of the scores of managers or entertainment lawyers who take part in the process, the major players are the driving forces at the powerhouse agencies. A handful of examples: Creative Artists Agency (CAA), Triad Artists, International Creative Management (ICM), William Morris Agency, Intertalent Agency, Agency for the Performing Arts (APA), and the Bauer-Benedek Agency. These entities and those like them are important to watch not only in terms of who they represent but also the movement of the agents themselves. You never know when the next agent is going to wind up as a studio executive. Still, before we attribute too much power to these agencies, we ought to remember that the ultimate success of the agent in getting the film made usually still depends on studio go-aheads.

Producers

Here we get into a bit of a problem of definition. I'll go into more detail when we address what I feel is my own unique take on the producer's varied roles. Basically, producers usually put together the elements that lead to completed movies. So, of course, within this profession is where we'll find a heavy concentration of buyers for what you have to sell. The trick is knowing how to weed through the scads of names of those who operate at all the different levels of this loosely defined role.

Given that there are innumerable small to middling production companies—some of which may have yet to mount a movie on the screen—it helps to distinguish them from the longer established independent producers and companies with real moviemaking power. For example, a few production companies you might recognize are Carolco Pictures, Imagine Films Entertainment, Largo Entertainment, Indie-Prod, and Lucasfilm, Ltd; others are Amblin Entertainment, Jaffe-Lansing Productions, Simpson-Bruckheimer Productions, Silver Pictures (Joel Silver), and Stonebridge Entertainment (Michael Douglas). Again, this drastically narrows the buying field since the distribution capabilities of the studios are practically a prerequisite to ever having a film seen. In other words, while an independent producer can both buy your project and even shoot it, most frequently a studio will still become involved as they have the strongest distribution relationship with movie theaters. I should add that an abundance of "independents" are either housed right on the studio lot or have what's known as a "first look" deal with a respective studio. What we're seeing so far is that, all in all, just about everyone in Hollywood is to varying degrees joined at the hip with the following bodies of power:

Studios

Universal Pictures. Columbia Pictures/Tri-Star Pictures. Warner Brothers Pictures/Lorimar Studios. Paramount Pictures. Twentieth Century Fox Film Corporation. MGM/UA Communications Company. Walt Disney Pictures/Hollywood Pictures/Touchstone Pictures. Orion Pictures.

Each of these studios has its own group of executives who hold the reins on the entire industry. Their immediate subordinates, too, have a definitive influence on what gets bought and made and delivered to audiences.

It would be imprudent to spend time naming these individuals at this stage of our exploration. Not because there are so many to name. In fact, my rough guess says we're talking about fifty to sixty men and women throughout Hollywood who have managed to ascend the studio ladder; only a small fraction of these will ever be firmly entrenched at a given studio. Also, even if you knew exactly who these executives were, that doesn't mean you can get them to read and consider your material. The truth is, almost everyone in Hollywood can say no to your idea, but only a few can say yes.

This is where the game becomes the ultimate challenge. We have seen that out of this cast of thousands—the stars, directors, writers, agents, producers, and studio executives —only a few highly placed individuals are truly capable of giving a movie a green light. And, although in this sense it is true that Hollywood is indeed a small town, these are the very one hundred doors that are the most difficult to unlock. Why? Because without the next all-important ability none of your wares will ever be seen:

GAINING ACCESS

This may sound like the proverbial catch-22, but take heart. In the course of almost twenty years since I first encountered the ground rules, I've come up with an array of options that can remedy this difficult challenge. Further on, we'll talk in detail about both the more conventional and unconventional means of unlocking those doors.

Contrary to the old saw which suggests that success is based on who you know, I like to believe talent will out. Eventually, no matter how adept a person is socially, he or she will be judged according to what he or she has done. Perhaps this is a reflection of my personal style, which relies on a love for the work itself as opposed to a knack for social-izing or "doing lunch."

Yes, many people have made it in Hollywood as a result of fortuitous alliances, otherwise known as social connec-tions. Those stories that we hear about deals being made over tennis games aren't far from fact. And I do agree that most studio heads or producers prefer to buy a project from a friend or an established business associate.

There is, however, one thing that no Hollywood deal maker can dismiss. This incredible item can provide you with a winning ticket. It can get the magical golden key which unlocks the fortress gates, providing you with access to the game. When well employed, it can be your most potent play-ing device which not only carves you a permanent foothold but a victorious one at that. It will earn you equal opportu-nity employment in Hollywood, regardless of whether you live on a farm in Nebraska, a high-rise in Manhattan, or a bungalow nearby in Studio City. In what can all too often be a random game of chance, you can do amazing things in Hollywood, USA, when you are in possession of:

A GOOD IDEA

In a very moving speech at the Academy Awards not long ago, Steven Spielberg paid homage to the sometimes over-looked creative individuals without whom no one else in the industry would work. He was talking about the screenwrit-ers, the storytellers, the artists who craft the words and the plots which, in effect, are precisely what engage us as the audience. Taking his thoughts a step further, I'd like to add that behind every wonderfully written movie, behind every exceptionally told cinematic story, is a good idea.

It's my belief that good ideas are the seeds from which good screenplays and ultimately good movies spring. They are also a formidable source of power for advancement in the film industry.

This book offers you an insider's look at the wide scope of what ideas can do in Hollywood. We'll explore the world of ideas by focusing on the following areas:

1. Creating and developing ideas
2. Testing the marketability of an idea
3. Refining the ideas
4. Pitching, packaging, and selling the ideas
5. Producing the ideas; participation beyond the sale
6. Creative options; from ideas to professions

I happen to be very passionate about good ideas. And so is Hollywood. In the wild and unpredictable moviemaking gamble, your idea has the same promising chance of selling to a studio as does an idea pitched by a studio executive's son. (Well, almost the same chance.) In this game the gun is usually clenched in the hands of the few power brokers who run the show. With a strong idea, you can take control of the gun. You can call the shots.

CHAPTER 2
IDEA POWER

"Nobody knows anything."

—William Goldman on Hollywood, from
Adventures in the Screen Trade

I'm not the first and I certainly won't be the last to cite this line by screenwriter/author William Goldman, whose book I highly recommend as a comprehensive and riveting view of Hollywood. In examining the movie industry power structure, Goldman points out that no one is privy to knowledge that can completely and absolutely determine the final outcome of a film. And because of the other popularly held belief that you're only as good as your last film, everyone is engaged in a constant chase of this elusive elixir—the recipe for a surefire hit.

Because nobody really knows anything, nobody will shun someone recognized as having good ideas. Nobody can afford the luxury of passing on an idea before considering it seriously. The notion that everybody knows that nobody knows anything is also why I stress being passionate about your ideas. Your passion, enthusiasm, and conviction that your idea would make a great movie can become totally contagious to someone whose future depends on which films he chooses to make. What does the executive know? Maybe you know something he or she doesn't.

There are an infinite number of actual cases—box office

hits—in which a person with a screenplay or story or idea simply refused to give up. Belief in the value of your idea will fuel your persistence. You'll find that after fifty-seven rejections there will be that fifty-eighth person who buys the idea. And then you'll be on your way.

HAPPY HOLLYWOOD TALES

George Lucas was just a guy with an idea when he brought it in to Alan Ladd, Jr. The project became a turning point in the lives of both director and studio executive, dramatically enhancing their careers and fortunes. *Star Wars*, which blossomed from that idea, became the second top-grossing movie of all time (as of 1989) and altered the course of cinematic history.

Karen Hopkins was working in a bookstore in Westwood when, during the late seventies, we happened to strike up a conversation as I was paying for a book. From behind the cash register while counting out my change, Karen ran an idea by me. Her pitch was this:

• •

A man cheats on his wife, the first time he has cheated in fifteen years of marriage together, and the entire affair is accidentally videotaped. It is a comedy where the action hinges on how this man must retrieve the videotape or see his whole life destroyed.

• •

Together with screenwriter Charlie Peters, I went in to Twentieth Century Fox and we pitched Karen's idea for "Peep Show." Charlie Peters was given a deal to write the screenplay and Karen Hopkins, who gave me the original concept, was able to negotiate her first sale of an idea. She had gotten into the business. Before long she obtained an agent and began to write screenplays. Cut to the present day and you'll be glad to hear that Karen Hopkins has since sold several ideas and screenplays and has earned hundreds of thousands of dollars in the process.

Another example of someone who benefited from idea power is Mark Miller, who'd initially set his sights on being a television writer. When I met him, however, he wasn't working. And although he'd managed to attain some experience and some Hollywood connections, he was well aware of the difficulties he faced trying to break into the feature world. Typically, it's tough for television writers to make an easy hop over to writing for film, let alone trying to sell a movie idea on a one-line pitch. Mark had no background in features, nor had he sold any screenplays. What he did have was a great idea called "Jury Duty." Instead of a serious courtroom drama situation, such as that in *Twelve Angry Men*, Mark's idea played with the comic flip side, describing it as "Twelve Pissed-Off People" or "Police Academy on the Jury." We pitched it with this one-liner:

• •

What two words strike fear into every man's heart? Jury Duty.

• •

My partner, Ed Myerson, and I took Mark and his writing partner for the project—Shelly Goldstein—to Warner Brothers. It was there that Vice President Bruce Berman bought the jury duty concept. Mark Miller and Shelly Goldstein promptly received $75,000 to write the screenplay, launching them both into screenwriting careers.

We sold Mark's next idea with this one-liner:

• •

What is every father's worst nightmare? Your daughter's first date.

• •

The father in the story is so paranoid about his daughter getting into trouble on her first date that he literally tags along behind, following her every movement on the date. Nothing bad happens to his daughter. In fact, she has a perfectly normal, apple-pie kind of evening. Everything that can go right about a date goes right for her, while her poor snoopster father encounters every disaster imaginable. Originally called "Home by Midnight," this became the television movie "Dream Date," which aired on NBC in October 1989.

Although Mark Miller and I sold the idea to Warner Brothers, he wasn't hired to write the screenplay. That job eventually was given to writer Peter Crabbe. However, Mark received an initial $5,000 for the idea and then an additional $30,000—when the TV movie was actually produced. Mark has since garnered an excellent track record. He's gone on to sell other screenplays, work as a story editor on the sitcom "She's the Sheriff," and is consistently being hired by the studios for a wide range of projects.

Here's an interesting case in which I was able to sell two ideas for someone I'd never met. Steve Kaire is a writer living in Brooklyn who'd heard I was open to receiving ideas submitted on three-by-five cards. One of the ideas Steve sent involved a New York cop who teaches an unusual adult education class at NYU. I took the idea, called "It's a Crime," to Henry Winkler and his partner Roger Birnbaum sold it to Columbia Pictures. Gen LeRoy was then hired to write the script.

Steve's second idea stems from a premise in which a typical American family becomes involved with a criminal. I partnered with David Permut and sold "Adopt a Con" to United Artists. The script was then written by Judy Meryl and Paul Meyers.

Not to be stopped, Steve Kaire continues to call me regularly and pitch his latest concepts. To date, I have sold three of his ideas and Steve has earned approximately $50,000. His earnings will increase if and when any of the movies based on his ideas are made.

Yet another instance of someone who was able to advance her career with an idea is Marilyn Anderson. Having been told that I was pitching ideas, Marilyn brought me the following concept:

. . . .

A woman, desperate to meet a man, regularly attends funerals in the hopes of meeting an eligible widower. Lo and behold, she meets the perfect man . . . but just maybe he isn't so perfect. . . .

. . . .

This idea could be viewed as a Hitchcock-type comedy which, as we'll continue to observe, is a superb way of devising new twists on previously proven ideas. Marilyn's story sold to Henry Winkler's company, Monument Pictures, and is now in development at Paramount. Not only that, she has established herself in the industry and recently worked as a writer for the new Carol Burnett show.

The case of a Santa Monica karate teacher, Emil Farkas, illustrates how the sheer simplicity of an idea can be coupled with fortuitous circumstances—catapulting an outsider into the Hollywood game. Among many submissions of ideas this fellow sent me on three-by-five cards was one called "Police 2000" that caught my attention. The card read:

• •

What if there was a police unit operating in Los Angeles in the year 2000 fighting crime?

• •

He also described the four main characters who made up the police unit, none of whom, I might add, were particularly well drawn. The idea was reminiscent of *Blade Runner* and although I'd certainly been presented with similar concepts, I decided to give it a shot. Given that it sounded like a very expensive movie to make, I opted to pitch the idea to some network people with the distant hope it could sell as a one-hour dramatic television series.

I got it to producer Larry Thompson, who mentioned the idea during a meeting at ICM. The agents at ICM just happened to know that Ridley Scott, who'd done *Blade Runner*, was finishing up a movie with Tom Cruise. The word was that Scott might be considering doing some television.

As it turned out, Ridley Scott not only liked the idea but agreed to direct the pilot and produce the series. What's more, he became the executive producer for the show. It wasn't much later that my friend Emil Farkas opened up the trade paper *Variety* to find his idea being touted as the hot new project in town: RIDLEY SCOTT DOING A PILOT FOR CBS.

THE POWER OF SIMPLICITY

All of the preceding examples testify to the impact that a basic, clear, accessible concept can have on buyers in the business. When uniquely tuned, twisted, or turned, a simple idea is as good as gold in Hollywood. Check out the next concept for its simplicity:

. . . .

What is a parent's worst nightmare? Your kids have just won a rock 'n' roll contest and guess who's moving in?

. . . .

This was the caption placed on a poster that my former writing partner, David Simon, and I made to help pitch his idea called "Rock Around the Block" to Brian Grazer at Imagine Films. The story is similar to the popular *Bye-Bye Birdie* but with a contemporary setting. The idea suggests that the kids have just won some sort of MTV contest—the prize being that the rock group comes to live with the family for a week. Simple, proven in a previous form, the twist here is an update with ongoing implications for high comedy and a great rock 'n' roll soundtrack. Currently being written by Michael Swerdlick, "Rock Around the Block" was born from David Simon's simple one-line concept.

Another idea of David's is a response to the hypothetical question, "What would happen if Harry Houdini came back from the dead?" With the title "Harry's Back, an Escapist Comedy," this project has interested actor Pierce Brosnan.

I began to recognize the importance of clarity when I was employed as a reader and had to plow through piles of screenplays. Since I was interested in becoming a screenwriter, the opportunity to read scripts was a great training ground. It is something I recommend for anyone who wants to write movies. Many of the screenplays I evaluated weren't very good; to be blunt, some were awful. So I began to ask myself what specifically was wrong with the scripts. Why didn't they work? The answer was, most often, that the central ideas were either too vague or far too convoluted and complicated. It became obvious to me that before investing time writing more screenplays of my own, I should take a stab at crafting preliminary ideas and testing their appeal. Little did I know that soon I would be on my way to selling all kinds of ideas, concepts, and stories to the studios. Here are just a few of the concepts that sold:

. . . .

"CLASS CRUISE"

I read an article about a semester-at-sea program in which students sail around the world on a ship—a floating college campus. It was obvious that the students on these ships had lots of fun and I thought it would be an unusual setting for a movie. I pitched it to the studios as "Sex, Drugs, and Rock 'n' Roll on a Cruise Ship" and also "Animal House on the Ocean" or even "Lust Boat." It was ultimately titled "Class Cruise" and made as a TV movie, which aired on NBC in October 1989.

. . . .

"CLOSED CIRCUIT"

Inspired by a Hitchcock movie, I came up with what I described as a teenage *Rear Window*, in which a couple of kids witness a murder. Instead of using Hitchcock's device—a murder taking place in an apartment across the way and viewed through a window—the action in "Closed Circuit" hinges on a murder the kids have seen, a murder videotaped by closed circuit cameras in the apartment building. The Ladd Company bought the project, which then was pitched and successfully sold to Warner Brothers based on the simple tag of "a youthful *Rear Window*." Again, the novel twist of the VCR—technology that was new at the time—and the tie-in to a familiar Hitchcock classic were two elements that appealed to the studios.

· · · · · · · · · · · · · ·

"GOING FOR BROKE"

This idea from Gerald Hughes was about a man who hears his name announced on the radio as the winner of the radio station's contest. But first, he must get off the freeway and overcome all kinds of comedic complications before he can claim his money. We sold the idea to the Guber/Peters Company at Warner Brothers.

· · · · · · · · · · · · · ·

"THE BAND RUNNER"

A low-budget rock 'n' roll feature which I sold to Paramount. The premise: A rock promoter gets gigs for fake bands who pose as famous rock groups.

· · · · · · · · · · · · · ·

IDEAS VERSUS SCRIPTS IN HOLLYWOOD

Back in the early days of Hollywood, the studios hired writers and put them under contract. This meant that the writers were paid to write their own ideas, or ideas the studio commissioned them to write, or movie adaptations of novels. As you walked by the bungalows on the studio lots, you could hear the constant clicking of the typewriters—a symphony of contract writers at work. What we now call *development* did exist, although the opportunities for outside writers to sell to the studios were very slim. Back then it was a closed system, in which the studios only used the screenwriters they employed. The practice of an outsider pitching ideas for sale to the studios was virtually nonexistent. Needless to say, an "idea person" ranked very low on the totem pole.

It's my observation that the Hollywood system was drastically changed into one of pitching ideas—rather than one of sending scripts around—as a result of the infiltration of the studios by television executives. In television it was always common practice for writers to come in to pitch ideas for all kinds of shows. So, as more and more television execs gradually made their way into positions of power at the major studios, with them a more open and receptive attitude toward the value of ideas evolved.

A second change in the industry has also paved the way for idea power. In the heyday of the "spec" script, a writer wrote a screenplay on "speculation." Author Syd Field, for example, whose *Screenplay* and its sequels guided a generation of Hollywood hopefuls in crafting and selling their scripts, emphasized the writing itself as a means to a career. As did the industry.

Once the script was completed, the writer pounded the pavement trying to get an agent. After that hurdle was overcome, the script would be submitted around town until it was optioned. Then it would sit in development until the option year was up. All this would have remained the same were it not for the fact that suddenly too many people were writing screenplays. In the early 1980s Writers Guild began registering 25,000 scripts on a yearly basis, a jump up from the 2,000 scripts that had been registered annually in the previous years. The market was being flooded. The fortunate consequence was that a more even flow evolved between the development of ideas and the creation of screenplays. As in other industries, the buying patterns of movie executives took on a cyclical nature, from periods of acquiring only completed scripts to periods of paying for the ideas to be developed.

This doesn't mean that Hollywood loves development. In fact, it is generally referred to as "development hell." Why? Well, as far as the studios and producers are concerned, buying ideas for development spells more time, more effort, and more risk—without a guarantee that the movie will get made. On average, a studio would have to develop four hundred ideas to get ten to fifteen movies made. Contrast that with the average one hundred screenplays a studio would have to purchase to get ten movies made.

All these statistics notwithstanding, the fact remains that the studios have huge budgets for development. A good idea is a good idea and when they hear it, they just do not want to let it get away!

Such was my experience during the first days that I began going around town with "just ideas." At the outset, I met with resistance. Executives would frown and tell me, "Go home, sit behind your typewriter, write more scripts, and when you're finished, we'll meet with you."

Swiftly, though, I started to see genuine interest from executives who wanted to hear not just one, but many ideas. As I made the transition from screenwriter to someone pitching ideas to someone selling ideas, the world opened up. With all my ideas, I had the option of giving the executives the right to hire a writer of their choosing, as long as I was paid for the idea and was attached to the project. Personal experience was proof enough for me that Hollywood had embraced the power of the idea.

Remember, though, there is no magic formula that will make Hollywood lay down at your feet. The magic, in my opinion, is that ideas do sell and that ideas happen to be very easy to find. Where to find them is exactly what we'll uncover now.

CHAPTER 3
IDEA GENERATION

"No dirt movies, no snow movies, no period pieces."

—Jeffrey Katzenberg, Chairman of Disney,
on subject matter to avoid in Hollywood

As you begin to cultivate the fine art of finding ideas, you'll soon discover that some ideas are not as welcome as others. This doesn't mean a less commercial idea is bad and should be discarded. It will, however, take longer to sell. The quote above shows that Hollywood has definite guidelines about the kinds of ideas that are not good. On the other hand, Hollywood has set no stringent rules on what makes a good idea. And this is where you, your instincts, and your ingenuity come in.

When, intuitively, you think you've struck upon a good idea, you just might be right. In my mind, the moment of discovery of a good idea often comes from a subtle combination of things—an instinctual/inventive flash combined with personal taste, a critical awareness of the hot movies at the time, a knowledge of the tastes of movie executives, and an informed overview of the movie industry so that you sense where your idea fits in.

Given all these necessary ingredients, it's maddening to me when I hear people espouse that ideas are a dime a dozen. To those who really believe that, I'll underscore now and in capital letters:

IDEAS ARE NOT A DIME A DOZEN

If the value of twelve ideas was literally ten cents, how is it possible that one idea alone can generate millions of dollars? And it's just not true that ideas grow on trees or that they can be plucked from thin air. Were it as easy as all that, the buyers in Hollywood would get rid of the sellers and churn out their own ideas. (Thankfully, that doesn't appear to be happening any time in the near future.)

Another common misconception is that there are only seven actual plot lines existing in all of written, dramatic, and filmic history, most of which date as far back as the Bible. The shorthand version of this type of thinking is: There are no new ideas. While these opinions can be debated endlessly, they're really irrelevant in the film business. In short, if Hollywood really believed that there were no new ideas or stories to be told, the whole industry would come to a grinding halt.

So now that we've established that they aren't a dime a dozen and that ideas can be new or original, the next question is:

WHERE DO IDEAS COME FROM?

In reality, they come from everywhere and anywhere. As I noted at the end of the last chapter, ideas are relatively easy to find. The trick to making the process easier, however, involves two skills that must be mastered. The first skill is simply an ability to *recognize* an idea as it occurs; the second and more difficult knack is in knowing how to *shape* it into a form that will sell.

A distinction should be made here between ideas created almost solely in your own head and those gleaned from outside sources. Although the end result—an idea—is the same thing either way, it's important that you not limit yourself by feeling you don't know how to "think originally" or "come up with something" on your own. I happen to think that very few people are truly adept at doing that. The following techniques, tools, and supportive materials are presented as ways to spark ideas. None require that you devise an idea that is totally original. If you do stumble onto something incredibly unique, that is icing on the cake!

The Blank Page

Most people who are serious about this pursuit have developed a discipline in confronting the blank page. One approach is to sit down at least once a week and stare at that untouched sheet of paper with an assignment to jot down a list of movie concepts. Start by asking yourself what kinds of stories interest you—what would you enjoy watching up on the screen? Don't censor your thoughts or be critical of ideas that might appear to be too close to concepts that have already been done. I'll emphasize throughout this book that Hollywood is a numbers game. So the more ideas you have, the more likely it is that one of them will hit. By forcing yourself to routinely write down your thoughts, hypothetical story questions, or the one-liners that we'll examine further on, you'll be amassing dozens of ideas.

Another way to deal with the blank page is to use a traveling notebook, journal, or diary. It goes wherever you go, for easy access. As ideas arise, grab that notebook and commit them to the page. A funny visual you might see, an odd situation, something provocative that someone says to you in the grocery store—all these everyday occurrences are fair game for your idea notebook.

Like a photojournalist who is always prepared to snap a picture, you'll want to make sure that you're always "idea-ready." If you saw Woody Allen's *Crimes and Misdemeanors*, you'll remember the character of the producer/director played by Alan Alda, who no matter where he was constantly came up with project ideas that he immediately verbalized into a microcassette tape recorder. Laugh as we may at such a show biz stereotype, it's a great device for listing and documenting ideas.

At a certain point, whether you've been working with a blank page or traveling notebook or tape recorder, you may find yourself starting to repeat those same dozen or so ideas. Maybe the ideas are becoming lackluster and you're just feeling stuck. From here, and in regular conjunction with the blank page approach, you can head directly to your friendly librarian. Or possibly even to your own bookshelf. . . .

Novels

Extracting an idea from a novel without adhering too closely to the full story is a fine technique for dredging up your own ideas. Pay attention to the various subjects, characters, and plots and see if that doesn't make you more aware of stories. What may result is enough of a twist on a story that you can end up with something new of your own.

If, on the other hand, you want to adapt the novel as it is, you must try to option it. Call the subsidiary rights division of the publishing company and inquire as to whether the rights are available or not. Very often, except in the case of a bestseller, you can option the book quite reasonably.

Although studios are generally hesitant about buying dramatic stories based on a pitch, they'll be more receptive if this is one that has proven successful in another medium. In the case of the book form—where an editor and a publishing house have already taken the gamble—a studio executive doesn't have to feel so much at risk.

Reference Guides

When it comes to plundering from the pages of these infinitely helpful resource books, you don't want to censor your choices of subject matter. The wider the range of topics you peruse, the greater the potential for uncovering ideas. From a basic encyclopedia to the yearly almanac, from the latest *Who's Who* to the more specialized directories of information, the fascinating facts they contain should provide you with fascinating film premises.

At the end of this book I have included several lists of research options—standard reference guides found in libraries and current texts which have recently hit the bookstands. When employing these materials as springboards to ideas, feel free to adapt and to play with the subject matter. The entries that are especially appealing and new to you will likewise probably make for subjects that are appealing and new to audiences.

The next category for reference guides deserves special mention since it can be particularly helpful.

Film Books

I recommend flipping through foreign film books as well as viewing foreign films. By going straight for the books, though, you'll get a speedy overview of both the successful foreign films and the ones which have not already been adapted as American films. Many great movies made in other languages are yet to be tapped, a process which Hollywood is happy to embrace. Following in the footsteps of a major hit such as *Three Men and a Baby*—a remake of the French film *Three Men and a Cradle*—your idea for a foreign film remake is going to be attention-getting. Once you've drawn from books on foreign films or on foreign filmmakers, rent videos of the ones that were of particular interest to you. And if you are truly entrepreneurial, go take a look at newly released foreign films.

Another gold mine which I strongly urge you to investigate can be found in film history books. Books on films of yesteryear along with the films themselves can give you a crash course in how premises have been developed throughout the history of moviemaking. What's more, you are at liberty to take a premise that has been treated in one fashion and give it your own ingenious twist.

My concept for "Closed Circuit" was generated in such a manner. I'd been thinking about ways to deal with topical technology and current trends when the idea struck to do something with what was then the latest nifty invention— VCRs. As far as the idea-finding process goes, I'd accomplished my first task; I'd recognized a thought as an idea. My job then became to give it a shape, a story form or context. Why not, I wondered, hook the VCR idea up with a classic murder mystery? Hence came my choice of an updated, teenage version of the classic *Rear Window*.

As you can see, ideas evolve through a variety of elements working in tandem. Start with your favorite films and ask yourself what plot elements you like in those movies. Then go to your factual reference sources and see what happens when you merge favorite movie remake ideas with unusual subject matter. You'll find a limitless number of potential backdrops for movies.

In your search for arenas, gear your information gathering toward up-and-coming trends. As shown in the case of the VCR in "Closed Circuit," being timely with your material can better the odds that your idea hasn't been pitched before. So look for the latest inventions, for new phrases or lingo, for topical concerns, social issues, and buzzwords that are just entering the mainstream. It is a common fallacy to think that because an idea is so new or unknown, nobody will care about it. On the contrary, audiences are riveted by stories they've never heard about before.

The other myth which we discussed earlier is that there's nothing new under the sun. I strongly disagree. New values come into our consciousness; new ways of communicating filter into our language. Events are happening that have never happened before. Take, for example, the fall of the iron curtain and the Berlin Wall and the freeing of Nelson Mandela. New stories are emerging about things we've never heard before. Divorced parents are kidnapping their own children. Greta Rideout sued her husband for rape, which marked the first time that the word *rape* was used in the context of a marriage. Next came the term *date rape*. Out of all these events, big and small, triumphant, tragic, and humorous, come ideas . . . and movies.

As to where to look for news, the answer should be fairly obvious.

The Media

Suppose you're browsing through *Time* or *Newsweek* and you read a story about airline courier services. These make for a bit of topical trivia; not too many years ago couriers weren't at all prevalent. How about a suspense thriller using the character of a courier? Why not? Had you not read that article, you might not have come up with this idea, which has potential for humor or suspense. Without regular exposure to media—such as magazines, newspapers, and radio and TV news—it's impossible to be aware of all the incidents and situations that are out there just begging to be forged into filmic ideas.

Keeping up with news that happens off the beaten track is another productive avenue to pursue. A member of my own family brought me an article from a paper I might have otherwise missed. It told of a new trend in Las Vegas whereby casinos were building hotels with dormitory areas designated for kids. It triggered an idea for a teenage *Ocean's Eleven* in which a group of kids comes to Las Vegas with nothing to do—so they rip off a casino. Calling it "You Ruined My Life," I sold the idea to Disney and it aired on ABC.

Also in a newspaper, I read about an airline losing someone's luggage. Not exactly the most extraordinary occurrence, this incident was made unusual and macabre because the luggage was a coffin. This kind of event can be hilarious when treated as a black comedy. The hunch that I could successfully convey that to an executive proved right when I teamed up with writer John Kostmayer and sold MGM the idea for "Where's the Body?"

By reading small-town newspapers, you'll no doubt come across true stories which can be fictionalized. If you happen to live in a small town or have access to newspapers other than those of New York and Los Angeles, you'll be at a nice advantage since you're reading stories that differ from articles being read by movie executives on the coasts.

Try researching back copies of various periodicals stored on microfilm in your local library. Going through old magazines for interesting or provocative stories will provide you with several options. You can alter the story, making it a fictional situation, or you can decide to buy the rights to the true story. You may uncover a true story already in the public domain—which means you don't have to buy the rights. You now own the idea by virtue of the fact that you discovered something others overlooked.

Later on, when I'll explain how I sold some other projects based on newspaper articles—"Back Flip" and *In the Mood*— you'll be given more specifics as to how you should proceed with ideas culled from the news. What I will say for now is that my first investment on the very project that got me into this field was twenty-five cents. In return for the mere cost of a newspaper, I was quickly on my way to becoming a producer.

A Secret Agenda

This approach to finding ideas is not so much a technique as an attitude. By realizing that you have a plan—that you're committed to finding ideas—all of your senses should be heightened. When you read a paper or watch the news, do so with a purpose. You're not only educating yourself or being entertained, you're doing the legwork that will bring you closer to your goals. As you open your eyes and ears and instincts to the world of ideas, you'll be quite surprised to find what's been surrounding you all the time.

Other people are wonderful resources for ideas. Look for odd characters whose stories might be the basis for a film. Listen carefully to others. Everyone has something interesting to relate—anecdotes, weird jobs, even inspiring accomplishments. And because you have a plan, you can specifically draw people out by asking them about themselves or about strange and offbeat events in their lives.

If your plan is not only to find ideas but also to sell them, begin to perceive life's ups and downs with a Hollywood point of view. Everywhere and anywhere, in the media and in your daily existence, always ask the question: Could this be a movie?

It's one thing to tell your friends that you'd like to be a Hollywood writer or producer; it's quite another to truly, physically, mentally live it and be it—twenty-four hours a day. I wish I could tell everyone that it's all fun, no work, and great perks. It can be fun and, yes, there are incredible rewards. But, truthfully, the Hollywood game is a lot of work and commitment. With a secret agenda to leave no stone unturned, you're going to be very busy. However, when that perfect idea turns up right under your nose—you'll spot it. The following examples of movies already made show how ideas come to those who look.

. . . .

SPLASH

Brian Grazer was driving near the beach, looking out at the waves. The thought occurred to him that it would be interesting to meet a mermaid. And the rest is movie history.

• • • • • • • • • • • • • •

DRAGNET

David Permut was watching reruns of the old "Dragnet" series and hypothesized about Dan Aykroyd in the role of Sergeant Friday. A movie was born.

• • • • • • • • • • • • • •

MIDNIGHT EXPRESS

Peter Guber read an AP news release about a young man who had been imprisoned for possession of drugs in a foreign country. He optioned the idea and ultimately a powerful film emerged.

• • • • • • • • • • • • • •

ENDLESS LOVE/SOPHIE'S CHOICE

Keith Barish came to Hollywood already a wealthy man but he wanted to be a producer. He connected with the William Morris Agency and optioned these two novels before they were to hit the bookstands. Soon both books became movies and Keith Barish had become a producer.

• • • • • • • • • • • • • •

Most of us can't afford to buy up rights to blockbuster books, but neither can we afford to shut our eyes to equally viable cultural possibilities. Local playwrights, small literary novels, offbeat articles—these areas depict contemporary subjects that if you don't exploit, you can bet that someone else in Hollywood will.

THROUGH THE HOLLYWOOD LOOKING GLASS

One of the best and most common ways to keep abreast of the kinds of projects that Hollywood wants is to read the trades—the daily or weekly issues of *Variety* and the *Hollywood Reporter*—available at bookstands in most major cities. Take note of what's being bought, optioned, developed, and shot. This will give you both a sense of the hot genres and also who is doing what.

Producer David Permut, for example (currently based at MGM/UA), has two projects in development that were found through very different means and differ greatly from one another in subject matter. I was able to talk to producer Pierce Gardner, who works with David, about the projects and how they were discovered. One of them, "Men of Respect," is a departure from *The Godfather* Mafia movies and is instead an exposé of the new Mafia. From a *Life* magazine article about a man named Francis, David Permut found the following story elements:

. . . .

A charming and handsome thirty-five-year-old who spoke excellent French, Francis had been arrested for having stumbled upon something bigger than prostitution, gambling, or drugs. As the ringleader, he had his new Mafia buying gasoline from different retailers, which was then driven across state lines and sold without sales tax. They were selling 600,000 gallons a week, saving approximately eight cents on the gallon of federal tax. Hundreds of millions of dollars had been made.

. . . .

David went to Europe to research Francis and then gave the idea to a writer with a twist to the story—a female cop is the protagonist who goes after the Mafia.

The other project in development that Pierce described is about Janis Joplin and is being produced with the music industry's renowned Clive Davis and Tri-Star. Eleven years ago, David bought the rights to *Buried Alive*, Myra Frideman's book about Janis, and since then has also acquired the rights to all of her music. In spite of the earlier film *The Rose* (fictionalized but based loosely on her life), her compelling story has yet to be fully explored on the screen. At the same time, Pierce takes pains to stress that it took Permut Productions a long while to get this Janis Joplin project going.

Smart producers and idea people track the interests of the stars who get movies made. Dennis Quaid had been telling people for years that he wanted to play Jerry Lee Lewis. Kevin Costner is known for his love of baseball, as proven by his work in *Bull Durham* and *Field of Dreams*. Take a tip from the producers who got the rights to the plays *Driving Miss Daisy* (with two tour-de-force starring roles) and *Steel Magnolias* (with its stellar cast of female roles) and be on the lookout for projects that will appeal to actors and actresses. You'll be in a great position if an actor or actress wants to develop one of your ideas.

Fertile ground for Hollywood idea picking is in the area of merchandise or properties that can spawn merchandising tie-ins. Over the past ten years, comic books and cartoons have become adored Hollywood commodities, yielding *Batman, Dick Tracy, Roger Rabbit,* and *Teenage Mutant Ninja Turtles*. These follow in the footsteps of films such as *Annie* and *Superman* and their sequels.

The producers involved in developing *Batman* were tilling fertile soil by coming up with something which obviously had merchandising potential. Studios know that there are millions of dollars of revenue to be derived from T-shirts, logos, toys, products tied in to the film, advertising, endorsement, and marketing opportunities—you name it. The next project that the *Batman* people are considering gains appeal from longtime popularity as an item of merchandise: a board game.

For years, various companies have tried to acquire the rights to Monopoly from Parker Brothers. If a movie based on this game is ever made, there will no doubt be lots of Christmas Monopoly game boards being sold on the tail of the film's release. The expected audience in this case is vast. Everyone who has ever loved playing Monopoly will be curious to see how it translates to the screen. Borrowing from this same approach, the movie *Clue* came from a popular board game of the same name. Likewise, I was able to obtain the rights to Chutes and Ladders from Milton Bradley and develop it as a TV game show.

There are products other than board games that inspire films. Currently in development is a movie based on the number one–selling doll, Barbie.

If you regularly read the trades, you've probably noticed that many movie projects are conceived by recycling or updating old TV shows. Ask a hypothetical question: What if the "Little Rascals" grew up to be the Big Rascals—with John Candy and Pee-wee Herman? Two ideas from familiar TV properties currently being turned into feature films are *Beverly Hillbillies—The Movie* and *Love Boat—The Movie*.

Also keep an eye on the topics being discussed on TV talk shows. If you're familiar with subject matter being raised by Donahue, Oprah, Geraldo, Sally Jessy Raphael, and others, you'll immediately pick up on the latest trends and timely social issues.

BUILD AN INVENTORY

We've heard the old expression that there is power in numbers, and this applies to Hollywood as well. Now that you have a sense of how to recognize and shape an idea, the next step is to do so in volume. If you have an opportunity to pitch an idea and it doesn't get picked up, don't be discouraged. Continue with your plan by building up a stockpile of ideas; none will ever really go to waste. Who knows? What doesn't sell today might very well become hot tomorrow.

Screenwriters and idea people live for the day when a studio calls up and says, "Gee, we loved your project. What else have you got?" When that happens to you, you immediately turn to all the other ideas you've been accumulating in your filing cabinet and get ready to pitch.

Success is a combination of opportunity and preparedness. Being prepared means having lots of ideas and a plan for what you're going to do with them. And that, in a nutshell, is the topic of our next chapter.

CHAPTER 4
SETTING YOUR SIGHTS

"Whether the motivation be glamour, fame, wealth or art, the movie business attracts the best and the brightest of America's youth, as well as a lot of the mediocre. But the individuals with the greatest ability are not necessarily the ones who succeed. What then are the traits that make for success? Hard work and tenacity are the two characteristics universally mentioned by industry veterans."

—From *Reel Power: The Struggle for Influence and Success in the New Hollywood* by Mark Litwak

We now diverge momentarily from our quest for ideas themselves and explain what you're going to *do* with the ideas once you've found them. Being too locked in on specific results can work to your disadvantage. Say you just want to sell your ideas and leave it at that. Fine. Say you've dedicated yourself to becoming a successful screenwriter. Excellent. But did you ever think about being a producer? If you have —that's terrific. If not, you'll be surprised to learn that becoming a producer isn't as formidable as you might think. Every time you generate—or find—a good idea, there's an opportunity to be a producer.

This is why, in seminars and lectures, I advocate both hard work and tenacity (as does Mark Litwak in the above quote), but I also stress flexibility. My advice is not to worry so much about what exactly you're doing on the road, but to just get *on* the road. Eventually you'll meet the right person who'll direct you to the right or to the left. Even if you are directed right when you should have gone left, you'll discover it for yourself and be that much more knowledgeable. Focus and perseverance will get you involved in the Hollywood process, but don't be deterred if you are led down an unexpected path. You never know, it may land you in a position that exceeds your original goals.

PLAY THE FIELD

My goal, as I mentioned earlier, was always to be a screenwriter. Then I began to find, pitch, and sell ideas, all with the hope of being given a chance at writing them. But when that didn't always happen, I was forced to conclude that if I wasn't hired as the writer on one of my own projects then I'd damn well better attach myself as a producer. If I didn't, I realized, I'd end up not making any substantial money on my own idea. And it was through just such a loss that I was made to face this reality.

In a 1944 *Los Angeles Times* article, I'd found the Sonny Wisecarver story. As a sixteen-year-old, Sonny eloped with a twenty-five-year-old mother of two. When his parents objected, the marriage was abruptly annulled—right in the middle of the honeymoon. A year and a half later, Sonny ran off with another twenty-five-year-old, the wife of a soldier and also the mother of two. In the forties, as you can imagine, this was a huge scandal, so it made for a provocative story idea. And when I interviewed one of the women many years after her interlude with Sonny, it was still clear from her description that the ladies just fell head over heels in love with this "Woo-woo Kid."

My partner, David Simon, and I tracked down Mr. Wisecarver in Las Vegas and offered him $500 for the rights to his story. Eventually, I made a deal on this project with Lorimar and David and I were hired to write the screenplay. My chosen career was well under way.

But, in time, David and I ended up losing the rights to our project. (It was later rewritten by Phil Robinson while David and I received a "story by" credit.) The picture was released as *In the Mood* with stars Patrick Dempsey and Beverly D'Angelo.

The misfortune was certainly not a Hollywood oddity, since screenwriters will often find themselves replaced by possibly several different writers before the movie is made. So I offer to you the lesson I learned the hard way: If ever you own the rights to a true story, *attach yourself to the project as a producer*. If you aren't hired to write the idea, or you're later replaced by another writer, that project will still be partially yours. A studio must keep you as a part of the production entity as long as you have the original rights specified in a proper contract.

Playing the field in this context means not being sold short or bought out cheaply. When I made the original deal on the Sonny Wisecarver story and the studio was willing to pay me and my partner $50,000 to write the script, that sounded like a tremendous amount of money. We were thrilled. What I learned later was the bleak fact that in paying us for the writing, the company had very shrewdly acquired the rights from us. Strictly speaking there should have been two contracts—one for the screenwriting deal and a separate one in which I would have given the film company an option on the rights I owned. This separate contract would basically have been for some form of producing credit. If the movie had not been made, then the underlying rights to Sonny Wisecarver's life would have reverted back to me. Unfortunately, I hadn't set my sights on producing—I'd glued my eyes on being a screenwriter.

And so I learned from the mistake not to think only like a writer, but to start thinking like a producer as well. It was this same principle in another situation that I consider one of my most fortunate breaks and most beneficial lessons.

This Hollywood case history also illustrates how twists in the path can lead to profitable discoveries and may prepare you for the different crossroads you might encounter.

Early in our writing partnership, David Simon and I pitched an idea to writer/producer Gail Parent who wrote for "The Carol Burnett Show" and is also the novelist of *Sheila Levine is Dead and Living in New York*, among other titles. Called "The Grapevine," our idea was for a situation comedy about kids in the sixties getting involved in publishing an underground newspaper like the *Free Press* or the *Village Voice*. Feeling enthusiastic about the idea, Gail took the two of us along to pitch it to then Vice President Brandon Tartikoff and Dick Ebersol at NBC. (Tartikoff wasn't yet head of NBC as he is today.) After the lunch meeting, which seemed to go very well, David and I had to ask each other whether we'd actually just sold something to NBC. Because our producer, Gail Parent, had been sitting there, no one had been crass enough to come out and ask, "Are you buying this idea?" Sure enough, the idea was sold and although the pilot script was never produced, David and I were happy to have a television development deal under our belts.

About a month or two later, we pitched an idea for a movie called "Scoop" to Disney. This was to be our first sale of an idea based on the use of a one-line pitch, which was, quite simply: *"Bad News Bears* set against the world of newspaper publishing." I want to stress, before we go into how to develop those one-liners, that while they're excellent selling tools, it's still important to provide prospective buyers with clear story elements and appealing characters. In this case, we had those ingredients, and in no time we found ourselves writing the screenplay in a big office at Disney with dueling typewriters. Before long, we'd pitched and sold a second idea to Disney called "Money to Burn."

With both scripts completed and ready to go at Disney, we encountered a sudden roadblock. Unfortunately, at the time, Disney was going through a great deal of executive transitions. We'd been hired during the Ron Miller regime, which was then replaced by the Tom Wilhite regime, which in turn would be replaced by the now famous and current Eisner/Katzenberg regime. Typically, incumbent studio heads aren't keen on "greenlighting" (putting into production) projects that have been bought by a predecessor. Although this isn't to say that the scripts absolutely deserved to be greenlighted, we were understandably disheartened when Tom Wilhite wasn't giving "Scoop" or "Money to Burn" (both bought during the Ron Miller era) the official go-aheads. To make our predicament worse, even though we had a contract at Disney, Tom was passing on the new ideas we were pitching.

In a pinch, we went to our lawyer, who quite fortuitously advised us to pitch our ideas elsewhere. How could we do that? After all, we were under contract at Disney. We could do it, our lawyer explained, because we were only under contract to Disney as *writers.* This meant that we could pitch and sell ideas to other studios as long as we informed them that we were not available as writers, that we were merely able to sell them the ideas. I immediately objected. Why would we want to sell our ideas without having a shot at writing them? That would mean we wouldn't be involved in the projects, wouldn't it? No, our lawyer pointed out, not if we became attached as producers.

I still didn't understand exactly how that could work, but I decided to give it a try. Within a year's time, I'd sold more than ten ideas around town while continuing to fulfill the terms of my writing contract at Disney. To my surprise, I found that when I pitched an idea to an executive and then went on to explain that my writing partner and I weren't able to write the screenplay, the executive's eyes would light up and a smile would appear. Studios were more than happy to attach me to the production entity, acquire the idea, and have it their choice as to who was brought in as the writer. What's more, I'd been lucky enough to stumble onto my

Hollywood destiny. I was someone with good, salable ideas, someone who was also known as a producer.

THE MANY ROLES OF THE PRODUCER

Before I am accused of oversimplifying the process of being attached to a project with a producing credit, I should mention that the first time took some guts. The studio executive blinked and said to me, "You don't know anything about producing."

"Fine," I said, "let me be a co-producer. I know a lot about 'co-ing.' "

And that's just what I did. Then, on the next project I sold, I was able to parlay the previous co-producing credit into a producer credit. Note here that you absolutely can't go into such a situation pretending you're someone you're not. You'll be immediately escorted to the door if you falsely promote yourself as some fabulous line producer who knows budgets and Teamsters and every camera angle. Tell them the truth: "I am not a line producer. But this is my idea and if you want it, you'll give me a producer credit." (This might be associate producer, co-producer, etc.)

It's helpful at this point to take a look at the distinctions between the extremely varied producing roles, so you'll understand that even when you are a producer on your idea, you may never step foot on the set.

The Line Producer

This is the individual who is on the set every day from before the first take to after the last shot. The line producer oversees the casting, the budget, and the locations, as well as coordinating with the unions and the entire crew. This is a hands-on job which definitely requires experience.

Many Hollywood producers don't physically produce the

movie in this sense. They'll hire line producers, while still receiving their producing credits and fees. Even the well-known producer of *Chinatown*, Robert Evans, who is known as a real hands-on kind of producer, doesn't work as a line producer per se.

The Executive Producer

As the title implies, this person is often the executive in charge of the whole operation and to whom everyone—including the line producer—ultimately reports. In some cases the position will go to the independent producer or individual who is primarily responsible for financing the film. Some executive producers are more interactive with the rest of the production team; others remain aloof during production.

Co-Producer, Associate Producer, Silent Producer, Producer

To avoid the many shades of gray that all such credited producing roles convey, let's just say each participates on some level in contributing to the creation of the movie and ultimately receiving profit from the movie—through fees and/or percentages.

It is within this range that you can negotiate a production entity credit. Were it not for your idea, the film wouldn't have been made. Everything else in the movie flows from your idea, so you are its creator and should be made so contractually when you sell your idea.

Realistically, however, without a track record or any screenwriting credits, you have to start lower than the rank of producer. You won't get very far demanding to be the sole producer or asking for a huge multimillion-dollar salary. Begin with an associate producer credit—usually given to the person who walks the idea into the producer's office—or as a co-producer, which often means you own the story rights. With a few of these credits under your belt, you can later negotiate a producer's credit.

David Permut is an example of someone who started out with ideas and segued into producing. Again, he wasn't a line producer with hands-on experience, yet he still retained the title of producer on his projects. His credibility as a producer came from having or finding good ideas—such as *Blind Date* and *Dragnet*. In addition to the projects of his we've already discussed, others on the current production/ development slate include one with Neil Simon and a project called "The Favor"—in which I am also involved.

David Permut deserves repeated mention in this book in that he typifies the aggressive producer's persona . . . he's an entrepreneur from the word *go*. Since he was a kid, David has been wheeling and dealing. As soon as his parents would leave the house on an outing, David would put up a sign on the front lawn saying TOUR JACK LEMMON'S HOME— $4.00. He was always fascinated by the movie industry and wanted to work in Hollywood. At the age of seventeen, David made an eight-millimeter movie and took it to a professor at Cal State. He was immediately advised, "Think about being a producer."

A couple of years later, he picked up a copy of *People* magazine with a cover story on Bill Sargent. The blurb read: "BILL SARGENT OFFERS FIFTY MILLION TO GET THE BEATLES BACK TOGETHER."

David was intrigued. Anyone who could get the Beatles back together, he reasoned, had to be one hell of an operator. This was someone David definitely wanted to know. And before long, he tracked down Bill Sargent and was able to get an introduction, whereupon he beheld the consummate idea man. David also discovered that Bill Sargent didn't have the fifty million dollars; he didn't have five thousand dollars. Bill Sargent had only an idea about reuniting the Beatles.

The embarrassing facts came to light when Sargent set up a meeting with George Harrison's lawyer in Los Angeles to pitch the idea to reunite the Beatles—via satellite. David's new colleague walked into the meeting saying, "I have a bona fide offer of fifty million to get the Beatles back together" and the lawyer looked at him and threw him out of the office. David said to Bill, "We're out of business!"

Bill's reply to David was, "We're just beginning."

All in all, Bill had come very far and had gained a degree of notoriety with this far-flung idea backed by nothing more than fantasy. And a few years down the road, Bill Sargent hit on an idea that really worked.

Having observed the growing numbers of comedians who were out there doing standup, he wondered: Why not film a standup concert on tape? Then the tape would be transformed to film and the "live" concert could be released in movie theaters. It had never been done, but Bill got to some backers in Texas and pitched his idea. He suggested that since Richard Pryor was playing the Santa Monica Civic Auditorium for two nights that upcoming July, the shows could be taped and released very quickly. He was given $400,000 to do the taping. Bill also went to Richard Pryor, explaining that since the concert was going to be taped anyway, Pryor could be part of the filming and editing process, which would ensure that the best material was released. Eight weeks after the concert, the movie was released. Called *Richard Pryor Live in Concert*, it went on to make $33 million!

While most of the money went to the studio, the backers, and Richard Pryor, Bill Sargent and his bravado won out. Witnessing these turns of events, David Permut now understood the true value of an idea person in Hollywood. He also saw that a true idea person was an oddity; no one else had the daring to promote ideas that seemed so off-the-wall.

David used that kind of daring and ingenuity in acquiring the rights and in selling his idea to do *Dragnet*. He first found out that Jack Webb's widow controlled the rights to the TV show and that she had in turn sold the rights to Universal. David unobtrusively bought the rights from Universal. After going to Dan Aykroyd and asking him to play Sergeant Friday, the two went back and sold the project to Universal. The studio wasn't too upset that David had sold them the very property which it had once owned. Why not? Well, *Dragnet* had just been sitting there all those years at Universal gathering dust and no one had seen fit to do it as a film. David Permut did and in the process made Universal $60 million.

Such an episode reveals that everything must be brought to the studios. They're not out on the street doing the job of finding every idea because they don't have the time. The studio executive's priority—first and foremost—is to see that projects which the studio already owns are getting made as movies. An outside producer can fill a gap by doing the hard labor and pursuing ideas.

POWER IN TEAMWORK

This brings me to another comment about the many roles in which a producer can function. At whatever level you enter the game, it's fairly safe to say that you can strengthen your stance with an ability to recognize other people's talents and to team up with them when the project warrants. Filmmaking is, after all, a collaborative process, so insightful producers will always be on the lookout for fresh, creative individuals—for their ideas, their writing skills, their unique visions—regardless of track records. By teaming up with talent, rather than seeing it as competition, you can better your odds in the Hollywood game.

One particular case in point was the very successful movie *Commando*. Seven years ago, I met Joseph Loeb III and Matthew Weisman, who at the time were two unknown writers living in San Pedro, California. One of the guys was working in a grocery store and the other was unemployed. We used to get together for hamburgers at a local diner and they would pitch me various ideas.

I knew when they pitched the idea for *Commando* that it

was a good one. Although I'm not an avid fan of this genre, I was well aware of the market for anyone looking to do another *Rambo/First Blood*–type project. It's common knowledge that Stallone and Schwarzenegger have seen every action script in town, so any submission to them has to have a strong gimmick or hook to make it unique. *Commando*, as you'll see from the following story elements, had a strong appeal.

. . . .

The protagonist's wife and daughter have been kidnapped. While holding his family hostage, the kidnappers put the hero on a plane to fulfill a mission he doesn't want to accept. In a very clever scene, he sneaks off the plane and sets his watch—because he knows that when the plane touches down and he's not on it, the kidnappers will kill his wife and child. In this "time bomb" approach, he has only so many hours to search the city for his loved ones. This gives him permission to overcome all odds by blowing away everyone in his path.

. . . .

This is what audiences love to see. If you can find a clever situation that gives the hero permission to blow the "bad guys" away, you've probably got a commercial idea. What was more, the two writers were very descriptive when they told me the story. I was sure this was a project that could be sold like a *Rambo*. So I started pitching it around and although I was very close to selling it, the writers decided to go ahead and write the script on spec.

After Loeb and Weisman finished the script, I proceeded to show it around. I took it to New World, Interscope, and then to Joel Silver—known at the time for *48 Hours*. Joel was a smart choice. His reputation with action/adventure was already excellent and he'd worked with Larry Gordon, then president of Fox and now head of the Japanese-backed Largo

Entertainment. Joel called me and said he liked the script, whereupon he got it to Larry Gordon. The two managed to get it done as Arnold Schwarzenegger's very next film—even though Arnold had several pictures lined up and ready to go.

In the meantime, my partner Stephanie Brody and I were given associate-producer credit and the two writers were catapulted into successful careers. They are now represented by Triad, have a writing/producing deal at Disney, several other deals throughout the industry, plus a backlog of credits including *Teen Wolf*. And whereas they used to pitch their ideas to me, I now look forward to pitching them my ideas.

COMMERCIAL HIT STRATEGY

I used the *Commando* saga to illustrate the importance of trust, patience, and collaboration with other people's strengths in your endeavors. It also proves another vital point in this process of finding your niche in Hollywood. As shown with the two *Commando* writers, one of the best ways to make the break is to do it with commercial material. Arlene Sarner and Jerry Leichling—the writers of *Peggy Sue Got Married*—knew that the genre of time travel fantasy was popular and their script attracted Kathleen Turner as the lead and Francis Ford Coppola as the director. Not a bad way to start off in the business.

All this doesn't have to mean you're going to get pigeonholed into doing only surefire commercial projects. But before you're given the freedom of choice to do what you'd like, you need that first commercial calling card. This isn't about "selling out." It's about selling smart.

If you study the accomplishments of today's prolific screenwriters, directors, and producers, you'll often see a commercial hit at the inception of their careers. Even the most successful examples that follow usually had to wait before they could make the projects truest to their hearts. In the meantime, they made names for themselves.

Woody Allen is certainly known for artistic individualism as a writer and director. But before he was able to make films like *Annie Hall, Manhattan,* and *Interiors,* he began with earlier commercial properties such as *Take the Money and Run* and the James Bond parody *Casino Royale.*

Martin Scorsese bought the rights to *The Last Temptation of Christ* ten years before he was given an opportunity to do it. In the course of that time, he made the high-concept picture *After Hours* first.

Platoon was a very similar situation for Oliver Stone, who had written it in 1977—ten years prior to its being made. And for Richard Attenborough, it took twenty years of his life to be able to finally make *Gandhi.* Even though major stars were interested in playing the lead, the industry took two decades to give Attenborough a go-ahead.

Tony Bill is the epitome of a multitalented entrepreneur who established himself commercially and has now earned artistic freedom. He has also fortified his success by having keen instincts in recognizing talent. Back in the 1970s, Tony was in somewhat of the role that I'm in now and was actively seeking out new writers. He would find the money and the company to back the script he wanted to do.

Tony Bill made the proverbial big break into the business by producing *The Sting.* It came from a first-time writer and went on to rank as one of the top-grossing films of all time. Having a nose for a talented screenwriter and a commercial property, Tony sold it and packaged it with Paul Newman and Robert Redford. He won an Academy Award in his late twenties, went on to do *Taxi Driver* and, among others, the critically acclaimed—though not commercial—*Five Corners,* written by John Patrick Shanley. With each successive project, Tony Bill is able to do movies that are farther away from the mainstream. Starting out commercially has given him that power.

HAIL TO THE SCREENWRITER

If it is true that most men live lives of quiet desperation, then producers live lives of active desperation. To survive, producers must hustle all the time. They are very open to meeting new talent—actors, directors, idea people—and they must be daily in touch with what's happening at the studios. But the cornerstone of their business is the writers.

Producer Pierce Gardner, whom I mentioned earlier, was told by David Permut on the day that David hired him, "Everything reduces to one rule. If you have good writers, you are a good producer. If you have bad writers, you are a bad producer. All the high concept in the world . . . all the great ideas in the world . . . nothing is going to make it work for you like a good writer will."

If your heart is set on honing your craft as a screenwriter, then I strongly recommend that you concentrate on two main areas. First, don't give up on writing your screenplays. And second, develop as many ideas as you can to back up your writing—to be able to pitch at the drop of a hat. You'll get a clearer understanding of why this is so as we explore various scenarios involving the roles of the writer.

Our first example is Dale Launer, a writer who by no means fits into the Hollywood scene; he doesn't even have an agent. Dale is very bright, very acerbic, and not an easy guy to get to know. You have to be direct with him and you have to deliver.

For some time, David Permut had been cultivating a relationship with Dale, who had sold his screenplay *Ruthless People* to Columbia. Permut, of course, was interested in any ideas Dale might want to pitch. Finally, Dale brought him an idea about a blind date, based on a true story about a hairdresser he knew. She was a great gal, but when she got drunk she became truly crazy. Then Dale informed David that he wanted to go to all the studios with the idea and to sell it for $125,000. That, Dale insisted, was his bottom line. At this point, although Dale had sold the one screenplay (which was being read as a sample script), *Ruthless People* hadn't even been made yet.

It was an outlandish demand. $125,000 for an idea! What nerve it took for Dale to propose it to David, not to mention the gall of David to ask it of the studios. Some executives balked right away—way too much money for an idea, they said. Some studios loved it. A deal was made and Dale wrote the script, which was then rewritten by Blake Edwards. To commemorate *Blind Date*, Dale keeps the movie poster taped to the floor of his garage so that he can run over it every day.

This brings me to underscore the fact that glory seldom goes to the writer. Although studio executives will read Dale Launer's script, audiences usually have no idea who wrote the movie or came up with the story. Except for films by Woody Allen and Neil Simon, there are very few movies people dash off to see because of the writer. What draws viewers are the stars, word of mouth, the impact of the advertising. You don't hear the average moviegoers raving about a "Dale Launer" film; you hear them talking about a comedy with Bruce Willis and Kim Basinger.

Rick Pamplin is a screenwriter who has many insights into the perks and pitfalls for writers in Hollywood. In addition to having written for many years, Rick teaches screenwriting at various universities and has invited me, upon occasion, to lecture in his classes. Our approaches were very different—Rick's was script-oriented and mine, as you know, was oriented to selling ideas. Rick thought I was basically just talking a good game, but before long some of his students pitched ideas to me that actually resulted in deals. Within the same time frame, Rick suffered a big disappointment with a deal that fell through on a script he'd been writing for six months.

What he was also soon to discover was that writers' scripts weren't getting read; they weren't getting past the readers. Over lunch one day with Carolyn Pfeiffer—then the president of Island Alive and now co-chairperson of Alive Films —Rick asked her how many scripts she received per week. The answer was two hundred unsolicited scripts. Rick asked if she read them herself. No, she explained, she hired readers. They were mostly college kids who would read a script for $25 and write out a summary with comments. Did she read all those reports? Again, no. Carolyn had an assistant go over the summaries. And every Friday afternoon her assistant would come to her office for forty-five minutes to pitch the screenplays she liked in little paragraph pitches.

The conclusion that Mr. Pamplin made was that if such was the destiny of a script on which you'd worked for six months, you'd better not pick the wrong idea. Better yet, why not start with a verbal pitch in that paragraph format (the way it would eventually be presented anyway) and sell *that* first? If you don't find any takers, fine. At least you haven't wasted your time developing it into a script. If they do want it, either sell the idea to the studio *or* sell it and fight for the right to write it.

This, let me point out, is a tough call. Depending on how good the idea is and what kind of experience you have, you can have the upper hand and get to write the movie. But you have to be willing to walk away from the deal.

THE FIRST DEAL

The hardest thing for you (and other budding writers) is to write that first first-draft screenplay of your idea when you've never sold a script before. You'll be up against many obstacles, but the most common is the sheer comfort factor that studios have with using writers who've worked for them before. You will be paid money for your idea and money *not* to write the script, just so the studio feels at ease. That's great as long as you've got lots of ideas. If this is your one hot, personal, unique idea and you're dead set on writing it, make sure you know in advance that you aren't going to give it away. Make sure, in this case, that you have some sample writing (one completed screenplay) and that you look carefully at the fine points of packaging, which we'll cover later on. (Should a middleman, such as myself, be able to get a star or a major director attached to your idea, your liability as a first-time writer will be diminished.)

David Silverman and Rogena Schuyler, two writers in Rick Pamplin's class, did manage to get hired to write the screenplay of "Stepping Out" for DEG. It is now in active development at the Guber-Peters Entertainment Company. These two writers are in a position to make a lot more money—a first draft fee, second draft fee, and then a big chunk of money should the film be shot. But more important than dollars is this critical event: They have made their first writing deal; they've entered the business and have that important first credit.

Without that credit, writers are kept as the outsiders of Hollywood. With it, you're given a pass to join the insider's club. When your name is listed among the actual on-screen credits, you'll have more leverage on your next deal, regardless of how successful the movie is at the box office. *In the Mood*, by the way, wasn't a commercial success, although it did do well with the critics. If your first film turns out to be a huge gangbuster of a movie, of course, you'll have everybody and their brother breaking down your door. Otherwise, it doesn't matter how well the movie does. What matters is only that you have survived the screenwriter's ultimate test—the first deal.

KNOW YOUR STRENGTHS

There is a moment of truth everyone has to face when hoping to sell an idea that you want to see become a movie. Ask yourself if you are really the best writer for your idea. If you can answer yes wholeheartedly, then go for it. If another writer who is more established than you can write your idea and make the difference between the movie getting made or not, you might consider giving your project to another writer. There are many people who can claim that they've sold scripts, yet only a fraction of those can say their projects were made. Shoot for being among the minority.

THE AGENT'S ROLE

It's known as the proverbial catch-22. To get most of your material submitted around town, you need an agent. But to get an agent, you need to have acquired some sort of success. So how can you jump this common hurdle? Well, there are a few different tacks that can be of help, especially if you have a completed screenplay.

In the back of this book, you'll find addresses and phone numbers for the Writers Guild. Contact the guild and ask to be sent a list of literary agents. Some of these agents will read unsolicited scripts. In writing your cover letter (and in all communication throughout the industry), the key words are: *concise, succinct, to the point.* One of the most erroneous beliefs some writers have is that quantity will be judged as quality, as if being able to write a six-page letter proves an ability to write movies. The opposite is true. The best way to grab an agent's attention—to make sure your script will be read and considered—is with a short, hard-hitting paragraph or two about your enclosure. When, further on, we talk about story elements, you'll want to take note of what highlights to describe in your letters to agents.

Most people agree that a first-time writer is bound to get lost at the bigger agencies. Even if you have written a brilliant screenplay, the bigger agencies are well stocked with their own stable of working writers and aren't as motivated to hustle on your behalf. The reasoning here is that a smaller agency is as hungry as you and will push your material more aggressively. These newer agencies are establishing their credits at the same time that they're establishing yours.

The diverging opinion is that any small agent who is willing to represent you as a first-timer isn't an agent worth having. Should a less proven agency be interested in signing you, it behooves you to find out as much as you can about the agents on board. What have they sold? How many writers do they represent? What kind of relationships do they have with producers and studios?

I know some writers who maintain that you're much better off going out there, getting a project sold yourself, and then finding an agent. Call up the reputable agencies and say, "Hi, I just sold something myself." Most will be happy to take you to lunch and discuss your representation. It's far better to shop for an agent in this manner. After all, you're walking in with a deal and making them money before they've even gone to work for you.

Bear in mind that an agency does two things. Agencies are responsible for both submitting your work and for negotiating the deal. As far as submission goes, there are alternate routes to be followed, such as submitting to smaller production entities or to individuals like me. As to the issue of negotiation, you can always obtain an entertainment lawyer to handle your deal. Some well-connected writers prefer to just use a lawyer—and some deals are so complicated that you'll wind up needing a lawyer in addition to your agent.

You may wonder how agencies feel about ideas, and the answer is two-sided. While I'd be surprised to hear that you were signed by submitting only your ideas to an agent, you can better your chances at being signed by letting the agent know you've got several ideas in addition to your screenplay. And also, by partnering your idea with another writer who already has an agent, that agent may be smart enough to sign you as well. I've said it before and I'll say it again: No one in Hollywood can afford to overlook the potential of an idea or an idea person.

I hope our exploration has given you a broader outlook on making your professional choices. Before we head back to honing the ideas, I have some last words of advice. Wherever you are and however you can, immerse yourself in the world of movies. Be persistent and never give up. Regardless of whether you're best with ideas, with writing, with producing—or all three areas—be aware that creativity and business are not mutually exclusive. The heroes of Hollywood use their artistic *and* their business sides to the utmost advantage.

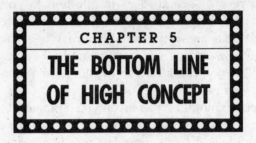

CHAPTER 5
THE BOTTOM LINE OF HIGH CONCEPT

"How do films get made? It must often seem to the film-maker trying to get his picture financed that there is no rational answer to this question. Somebody, somewhere says yes or no to an idea for mysterious reasons that seem to have as much to do with gastric indigestion or life at home as with the intrinsic merit of the project. And, in fact, there is no cliché answer to this cliché—if all important—question. There is no ready formula, no list of qualifications I can give you. Whenever somebody comes into the office and asks us what we are looking for, the only answer we can give him is, 'Something good.'"

—Interview with David Picker, "On the Distributor," from *Movie People*, edited by Fred Baker with Ross Firestone

In the course of being interviewed for the *Los Angeles Times*, I recalled to writer Jack Matthews that back in my rookie days I'd heard how Joan Didion and John Gregory Dunne had sold *Panic in Needle Park* by pitching it as "*Romeo and Juliet* on drugs." I remembered thinking, "Hey, I can do that."

As I also explained to this interviewer, the thing I loved most about movies when I was a kid was being able to leave the theater and then go tell someone else about the story. I would attempt to enthrall family and friends with my movie reenactments. What was particularly interesting, considering what I now do, is that even way back then, I could retell the story in a very short amount of time by boiling the movie down to the most exciting points. I've likened the ability to "Name That Tune." You know the game—"I can name that tune in three notes." Well, in this respect, I can describe a movie in three lines. And sometimes, like Joan Didion and John Gregory Dunne, in less than that.

What marketing experts in Hollywood have found is that a movie that can get everybody telling their friends the story, who in turn will go to see it and tell their friends, is going to be a hit. So the marketing people are very keen on doing movies that lend themselves to succinct descriptions. Likewise, when you go to pitch the idea to the studio, you should have it honed into that simple, compelling shape. To truly fathom the mind of a studio executive, you'll need to know the answer to the following question:

WHAT IS HIGH CONCEPT?

Many people credit the derivation of the one-liner caption for high concept to Barry Diller, the current head of Twentieth Century Fox, and to Michael Eisner, who now runs Disney. In the late sixties, the two were at ABC working to promote the TV "Movie of the Week." To get forty million people to tune in to a TV movie without the familiar faces and story formats that viewers were used to watching on the regular shows, Diller and Eisner had to devise a way to grab attention in a *TV Guide* listing with just one or two lines. That's how the term *high concept* originated. To capture an audience, that one sentence had to convey just how exciting, sexy, provocative, and entertaining the movie was going to be for them to watch. See how the next high-concept idea grabs you.

• •

A deejay is terrorized by a woman who has fallen in love with him. Feeling betrayed, she decides to murder him.

• •

That, in case you didn't guess, was *Play Misty for Me*, which is the same premise used ten years later for *Fatal Attraction*.

The essence of high concept is that it is both brief *and* provocative. It piques the imagination and promises that big things are going to happen out of an ordinary situation. The idea that Tony Perkins gussies up as his mother in *Psycho* opens wide multiple possibilities for suspense. Provoking interest can be done in all genres. In the comedy *Some Like It Hot*, for instance, two men also dress up as women, with hilarious consequences. The same goes for the humorously provocative *Tootsie*, based on a similar device of "cross-dressing." High concept can be applied to comedy, drama, action/adventure, horror, and fantasy.

Out of the top ten movies every year, most of them are raised from a high-concept premise. *Twins* drew a lot of criticism for being high concept and was panned by movie critics for having a so-so script. The implication was that the movie was all gimmick and no substance. Yet *Twins* made over $100 million because audiences loved the concept of Arnold Schwarzenegger and Danny DeVito as twins who had been separated at birth.

If you break down the meaning of the term, the literal translation is that there is a high amount of concept in the movie, or that the concept is high above the rest of the movie's components. All of the action is hinged on that one critical point. It's sometimes referred to as a hook, a twist, or a gimmick. The hook in a song, for example, is the key line that is repeated throughout the song. When you hear that key line, you're hooked on the song. When you hear the hook of a movie, you should immediately know what it's about. You're hooked and want to see the movie. Or buy the project.

When asked how she would define *high concept*, one Hollywood screenwriter quipped, "Three lines and it's sold."

THINKING HIGH CONCEPT

Go back to those ideas you've been generating so far and see if there is a potential hook in any of them. The test is in whether you can describe a provocative movie in one or two lines. If someone else were to look at that one-liner and ask "But what's the movie about?" then you do not have a high concept.

The next stop is to breeze through a copy of *TV Guide* and read the one-liners used to describe scheduled movies. Try to emulate the style and structure of the *TV Guide* listings in executing your idea. You never know, you might be able to adapt the one-liners you find there into movies of your own. Similarly, the newspaper ads and poster slogans for movies at your local cinema can school you in how to word your descriptions. These blurbs are what entice audiences; they are publicity come-ons for the actual stories. Think about how you can make your one-liner a tease. Let us know just enough about the movie so that we're dying to hear more.

Blind Date provides a splendid blueprint for high concept —it's in the title! A good one, like this, tells you what the subject is going to be right up front. You won't need a treatment describing the plot; you won't even need to give a beginning, middle, or end.

Don't worry if thinking in high-concept mode doesn't come easily at first. Like anything else, it's a learned skill and so the more you play around with it, the better you'll get. It isn't the be-all and end-all in Hollywood, but rather a great tool for pitching. Try coming up with one-liners on existing movies, as if you were pitching them for the first time.

Say you wanted to pitch *Amadeus*. You could play someone fifteen seconds of the best composition Mozart ever wrote and then ask the question:

• •

Who would want to kill a man who makes this kind of music?

• •

Or how about *The Graduate*:

• •

How do you tell the girl you're in love with that you're sleeping with her mother?

• •

Let's look now at some other handy techniques to help you formulate your idea.

See How High It Can Go

Try the trick of taking your situation to the *n*th degree. What is the absolute most impossible wish for a character in your situation? The absolute worst fear? The kookiest, wildest fantasy? You want to take the premise from the original thought and exaggerate it to outrageous proportions. When you wonder whether or not you've gone overboard, use high-concept movies like *Ghostbusters*, *Splash*, and *Tootsie* as your measuring sticks. Check out this high concept and observe how it was most likely constructed:

• •

What is the worst thing that could happen to a babysitter? She loses the kids.

• •

From *Adventures in Babysitting*, of course, something like this could happen . . . and probably has.

Remember, when you're out there pitching these ideas, executives are looking at both how commercial they are and how unique they are. An idea should be *like* something successful that's been done before and markedly *different* at the same time. Alike yet different? Sounds tough, doesn't it? That's why it's important to use the next guideline.

Know How High Is Too High

There's a response sometimes voiced in the industry that an idea is too "over the top." This usually means that your idea is too different or too strange. If an executive has no reference point, no other movie to which it can be compared, then your idea won't be a viable prospect. If you give your one-liner and then have to spend twenty minutes explaining this weird concept that only a rocket scientist could understand, you have to head back to the drawing board.

To keep high concept at the right level, be sure to test it first. Can you make it more *simple*? Can it be told in *one or two lines*? Does it conjure vivid *images* and *possibilities*?

A fellow came to me with an article about the phenomenon of "band runners" which had hit a few magazines, including *Rolling Stone*. Before looking at the article, I asked him what these people did. See if you think there's a clear concept here:

. . . .

A band runner, in this case, is a hustler, a con artist. The bands he promotes are fakes, such as a group of girls he hired who were lookalike Supremes. A band runner could potentially make tons of money fooling the public.

. . . .

I thought it was a very unique, interesting concept and a completely comprehensible one as well. I was even more impressed when I read the article. Anyone else could have had the same idea from reading it, but this writer was smart enough to pick up on it and pitch it first. When you hit on a good high concept, you know it—it leaps off the page. You'll ask yourself why you didn't think of it sooner.

Don't make the mistake of thinking that a wacky character is all you need for a high-concept pitch. Plug the wacky character into a normal situation and then you've got a premise. Or better yet, plug a normal person into a bizarre situation and then you're cooking. The odds are usually better for an everyday Joe or Jill to reign supreme with the audience. The leads in *Love Story*, for example, were generic enough for everyone to identify with them. (High concept means never having to say you're sorry.)

X Meets Y

Remember my project about a floating campus? By describing it as "*Love Boat* Meets *Animal House*," anyone can get the whole picture and everyone can laugh. I used the tag line "*Rear Window* Meets *1984*" when pitching Closed Circuit. By merging two contemporary movie titles that are immediately recognizable—X meets Y—you come up with a brand-new brainchild, a high-concept Z.

Another way to use this technique is to have two diametrically opposed characters meet. The sum of that equation will be action. The recent film *Internal Affair* has good cop meeting bad cop. This formula is used all the time in romantic comedies. X meets Y and they hate each other but by the end of the action they have fallen in love. In the literal example, *When Harry Met Sally*, he thinks she is uptight and she thinks he's obnoxious. After two hours of friction, however, they've recognized that they really love each other. And that's exactly what the audience was hoping would happen all along.

But please note that *When Harry Met Sally* is *not* high concept. It's two characters talking for ninety minutes, and that doesn't make for a good pitch.

What If?

I've mentioned this terrific method before and it is repeated because it is so useful for brainstorming before you get to the high concept. What if a baby talked? What if aliens landed near an old folks' home? What if you could travel back in time? *Look Who's Talking, Cocoon, Back to the Future* all took their concepts a step further with twists, but each probably started with something like a "what if" question.

Can You Flip the Genre?

In moments from now, I'm going to be rating the genres that do well in the pitch process. In the meantime, you can also come up with high concepts by flipping a high concept that worked before within one genre into another genre. Hitchcock's suspense film *Strangers on a Train* was flipped into comedy in *Throw Mama from the Train*.

Mel Brooks, for that matter, flipped several Hitchcock suspense thrillers into the comedy *High Anxiety*.

If you are dabbling with a movie from a particular genre, it may interest you that some films from the past are now in the public domain. To find out whether an older movie has come into the public domain, first try checking at the Academy of Motion Picture Arts and Sciences. Their research department may in turn refer you to the studio that released the movie, whom you'll want to contact by calling their business affairs department. After inquiring whether the underlying rights belong to the studio or whether they have possibly reverted to an estate, and if the answers are both no, then you should verify any action you've decided to take with a lawyer or your agent. (While this may sound like a laborious procedure, it will be well worth your while should you be able to obtain free rights.)

The technique of flipping genres, I might add, should be used with discretion. If the film you've chosen for your reference point is a recent dramatic release that didn't do well at the box office and you want to develop it as a comedy, you may achieve an interesting idea. However, I wouldn't mention the name of the unsuccessful film when you get to the pitch stage. On the other hand, if you're choosing a hot movie and you say, for instance, you're doing *Lethal Weapon* as a romantic comedy, most people are going to look at you and say, "Huh?" In fewer words . . . some genres don't flip.

On the Cutting Edge

Sharpening your high-concept idea so that it's on the cutting edge requires a very subtle sense that recognizes its timeliness. As we observed earlier, you can gain this awareness by picking up on trends that are just about to hit the mainstream. If the trend doesn't last long, you'll have a dull blade. If it's about to become a household phrase or a buzzword passing from coast to coast, then by the time your movie is released, you'll be in the forefront of movies dealing with similar concepts.

What can really make the difference here is our next topic. So now, before we get carried away in singing the praises of high concept, we should address the other essential marketing concern:

SUBJECT MATTER

By subject matter, I'm really referring to both the *genre* and the *arena* of a movie. A comedy set in the arena of business

—like *Working Girl*—is going to be very different from a drama, such as *Wall Street*, which is set in a similar arena. Regardless of how good the basic idea, success in pitching it will depend on the subject matter. Likewise, if you pick weak subject areas, it doesn't matter how brilliant your screenplay is. To echo the thoughts of screenwriter Mike Kane, who has said "Screenwriting is all subject matter," I'll add that the sale of your idea can hinge on this issue.

Writers who have sold one script and have been given a deal to write another will often come to me looking for ideas. Maybe they've run out of their own ideas or maybe they've just had a bad meeting with the studio executive. Usually what has happened is that the studio has pitched the writer various subjects that it wants to see written. This doesn't help the screenwriter; the writer needs a story—an idea that can be explored within that genre or set against a particular backdrop. When the executive says "We're interested in a murder mystery," or "We're interested in relationship pictures this year," he or she is tipping off the idea people as to what subjects are going to fly.

Genres can be broken down into many subgenres, but we're going to focus on the Hollywood garden varieties—the genres that are the most popular at the box office and, synonymously, with the studios.

Comedies

Given a few shifts every now and then, comedies will always rank at the top of the list. I, for one, am particularly interested in comedy, though certainly not to the exclusion of other genres. Mainstream comedy, which lends itself to a wide range of audience members and is very castable, is a sure bet. Romantic comedy is always marketable in that you automatically know you're going to have two big stars. Broad and outrageous comedies mixed with romance are the best; we all want to laugh about our follies in love. Sci-fi or fantasy done comically is terrific. Black comedy, with its more cynical edge, will pull in a smaller audience but it is nonetheless marketable to Hollywood.

Also hot are funny "fish-out-of-water" stories in which a character ends up in a world where he or she doesn't belong. *48 Hours* was an idea within this framework; Eddie Murphy belonged in jail but ended up out on the street—solving a crime with another cop. The high concept here, by the way, is hinted at in the title—Nick Nolte needs this criminal to accomplish his mission and they've only got forty-eight hours to do it. It's sometimes thought that this movie is a relationship or buddy picture, but its strength comes much more from the fish-out-of-water premise. The characterizations, no doubt, and their peculiar relationship were both wonderful. What really sells about *48 Hours* is the concept of a prisoner out of his element, acting like a cop.

Hollywood loved another film of Eddie's, *Trading Places*, which also was a fish-out-of-water story. As a scam artist, an unemployed beggar, the character is suddenly plunged into a penthouse Jacuzzi in Dan Aykroyd's wealthy world. Jack Nicholson in *One Flew over the Cuckoo's Nest* is a very sane man who, because he doesn't want to go to the prison work farm, is forced into the foreign world of the insane asylum. The quintessential fish-out-of-water story is *Splash:* a mermaid-out-of-water in a human world.

A variation on fish-out-of-water stories was dominant in the 1988 rash of body exchange comedies. You can't be much farther from your own world than a father who is living in his teenager's body.

Action/Adventure

Here is another preferred Hollywood genre, although your success in selling your idea will depend on how you make your story twist unique. If you have an action movie that can star a Mel Gibson, a Schwarzenegger, or a Stallone, and you have some angle on it that makes it different, then you'll have no trouble marketing this idea. A lot of action stories employ the hero myth, which we'll review shortly; some, alternately, are built as buddy films. In playing around with this genre, think *Lethal Weapon* and *Die Hard*. Try to impose a near-impossible time constraint within your concept—as if there were a time bomb ticking away.

Sci-fi/Fantasy

Generally, science fiction is expensive and can run the risk of being overly complicated. If you have a simple, accessible concept that a mass audience can understand, though, this is worth pursuing. The simplicity of the classic TV series "The Twilight Zone" is the measure of how far to go with a science fiction idea. If it is really esoteric and would only appeal to sci-fi buffs, then I'd pass on it. An example of a great concept for sci-fi is *Running Man*. In a futuristic society, Schwarzenegger must play a game show—if he loses, he's dead.

Taking a movie like *Honey, I Shrunk the Kids*—sort of a sci-fi/comedy for kids—you find out that the science isn't what's important about it. The actual mechanics of how the kids are shrunk is by no means what draws in the audience. The exciting, amusing lure for viewers here is the premise: microscopic kids in a world where even the most mundane household appliance is life-threatening. The pure simplicity of this movie has a one-liner as its title. Just picture the befuddled Rick Moranis saying, "Honey, I shrunk the kids," and you've already roped in your audience. The same goes for Lily Tomlin's *The Incredible Shrinking Woman*, which used the same basic premise, and for *Back to the Future*. The simplest of ideas in this genre are often the ones that can bring in a substantial audience so necessary for that first crucial weekend of a movie's release.

As you'll see when we review the top box office draws,

science fiction and fantasy score well when combined with comic elements.

Horror/Ghost Stories

The horror genre sells, as you can observe from its constant presence among new releases. It tends to have, however, a smaller market, unless it contains that all-important unique spin.

As with other genres, the best approach to choosing an arena for your idea is to turn the ordinary world into an extraordinary one. A promising ghost story begins with people in a mundane world, where their existence suddenly becomes perilously haunted. In *Poltergeist*, an average American family in a normal town find themselves terrorized when the tortured spirits of souls buried under their house come to seek revenge.

Murder Mystery/Psychological Thriller

When we cover the distinction between ideas best for film as opposed to television, you'll note that TV has mostly taken over the murder mystery genre. If yours has a truly novel hook or will be seen as being too explicit for TV, then go for it. The thriller *Sea of Love* works because of the unusual device of a song as evidence and because it's sexy and suspenseful enough to play on the big screen . . . not to mention a terrific script by Richard Price!

A murderous psychological thriller, such as *Fatal Attraction*, can also be built from transforming the ordinary into the bizarre. If you recall, in that film a run-of-the-mill affair turns into every man's nightmare.

Social Drama

This genre is tougher than others to sell with a pitch, although if it is incredibly provocative or ties in to topical issues, its chances are better. *Kramer vs. Kramer*, for example, picked up on a major trend at the time of its release. Some women who were newly seeking their independence were leaving their husbands—but who would take care of the children? This was a controversial new phenomenon and we hadn't seen it fifteen times before.

It's usually thought that social dramas are too small for the big screen. Whether this is absolutely true or not, I do know I wouldn't be able to sell a *Terms of Endearment* or *On Golden Pond* from a pitch. These are movies that rely on characters and dialogue to deliver the concept. On the other hand, if you have a social drama that has worked in another medium —in a play or novel—and has a big name attached to the project, you've got a good contender.

Real-Life Stories

Ideas based on true-to-life events are frequently bought as films or as TV movies. Films such as *Scandal, A Cry in the Dark, The French Connection, Gorillas in the Mist, Talk Radio,* and *Betrayed* are all—to varying degrees—based on real-life stories about real people.

Similarly, the more sweeping, fictionalized treatment of historical events or particular eras—as seen in *Mississippi Burning*—do find a Hollywood market. You'll observe in these cases that many bill themselves at the last roll of the credits as "based on true events." Further examples are *The Last Emperor, Gandhi,* and *Missing.* Down the road, I'll hash out in more detail just how to deal with fact and fiction.

Love Stories

This isn't a genre per se, but you can pitch it as such. The good news is that Hollywood always loves love. *Pretty Woman,* one of the sleeper hits of 1990, is a recent example. The difficult task will be making sure your story has a novel variation on the oldest theme in the world. "Boy meets girl" has been done so many times that you have to find a way for boy to meet girl that has never happened. If you've got a handle on it that is funny, startling, or scary—go for it.

Sequels

Sequels, you probably know, provide safe choices for the studios in that they offer a guaranteed audience. When we review box office history, we'll discover that several sequels have done extremely well. While I wouldn't recommend sitting down and only coming up with ideas that can be sequelized, your selection of genre can take future possibilities for sequels into account.

I mentioned earlier that the business has definite notions about what genres and arenas are not commercial. Slice-of-life films—like *Diner* and *The Big Chill*—are typically difficult to pitch. What can you say about them—that a bunch of friends get together and talk? Woody Allen's *September*, unless you are Woody Allen, cannot be sold from a pitch.

Still, as we look at the list of Hollywood no-no's, bear in mind that there are always going to be exceptions to these rules. If you are impassioned about certain subject matter, you may be able to present your idea in such a fashion that will assuage an executive's fears. Your story may be so riveting that troublesome subject matter is overlooked. You can also give a noncommercial subject a high-concept base that will give it marketing appeal.

Movies always harder to sell are those which deal with issues such as religion, racism, homosexuality, abortion, disease, terrorism, and international or complicated politics. For various reasons, it's wise to avoid backdrop or settings that involve sports, ugly or brutal physical environments, third world countries, and even stories set outside of the United

States. Remember the theory we saw before that is attributed to Disney Chairman Jeffrey Katzenberg: "No dirt movies, no snow movies, no period pieces."

The aforementioned settings are either unappealing to American viewers or expensive and uncomfortable locales in which to physically produce the movie. Westerns, along with films set in the twenties, thirties, and forties, as well as war movies are all looked at askance by marketing experts. However, the recent success of *Dances with Wolves* may change things. Epics, like a *Gandhi*, aren't easy to sell, especially not from a pitch. Veer away from arenas that require elaborate special effects, particularly those in outer space or on other planets that would cost $40 million just to construct the set. Hollywood only makes one or two of those a year and chances are that Steven Spielberg or George Lucas will beat you to the punch!

More don'ts: no white slavery, no Vietnam vets tracking each other in America, no religious cult groups. There are many people right now trying to pitch state-of-the-world environmental movies, which are not being well received by the studios. These have definite messages, but no stories. If the idea is based on a true story, that improves the situation and may be a viable contender—especially for a television movie. In the meantime, though, if your idea is based on the world as you'd like it to be, you probably won't find the market for it in Hollywood.

Believe it or not, the most commercial subjects right now are contained in stories about dogs, doctors, and babies. Strangely enough, I've seen a lot of ideas lately about animals turning into people. It's one of those mystical coincidences that at one time or another a certain idea will pop into human consciousness and a whole fleet of this type of idea will come marching into Hollywood.

The handy rule of thumb in going after subject matter is to ask yourself how many people with different social backgrounds, of different ages, will be able to relate to your movie. The studios are looking to make films that have cross-over appeal or that will attract a wide audience margin. It should come as no surprise that the majority of movies currently made are contemporary comedies set in urban centers about adults. Who can't relate? Subjects that are used in movies like *Tootsie, Splash, Fatal Attraction,* and *Three Men and a Baby* all combine with simple concepts to become immediately accessible. They feature characters with whom we can relate, who are caught up in extraordinary circumstances that are potentially real; conceivably, these extraordinary circumstances could happen to us. Family films are also getting hot, i.e. *Look Who's Talking, Home Alone,* and *Kindergarten Cop.*

One last consideration that can affect the choice of subject matter is the politics prevailing at a given studio or company. A change of executives, for example, will alter the production slate. There was a difference in the type of movies released by Columbia from when David Puttnam was in charge to when Dawn Steel was in charge.

Along these lines, studios may have scoped a particular campaign or agenda that will affect what they make. A studio might wish, for instance, to cultivate a relationship with a certain star or director and therefore be willing to take on noncommercial subjects. Presumably, this reasoning applied when someone like Warren Beatty was given the studio go-ahead to do *Reds,* which didn't exactly contain overtly marketable material. An exchange was implied; if he was allowed to do *Reds,* then maybe he'd come back and work with them on something else. It also works in reverse: A director will agree to first direct the studio's choice of material if he can then get a green light on the film he especially wants to do.

Sometimes an individual producer or head of a company will have a special interest in dealing with specific subject matter. *Parenthood,* as a case in point, was done by Imagine Entertainment when Ron Howard, a father, wanted to share this bittersweet experience.

To illustrate what an advantage you can gain by knowing what types of films are getting done where, I'll give you a brief tour of the kinds of choices that the heads of Imagine—Brian Grazer and Ron Howard—have been making. Like *Parenthood*, their movies are typified as contemporary mainstream comedies with *heart*. In other words, the material isn't as broad as in, say, *Police Academy*. Imagine's films make a statement about the human condition; they will contain a transformation of character. As an informed professional, you wouldn't go to them to pitch something like *Die Hard*. Their commercial success derives from offerings that include strong concepts married to marketable players. What's more, they don't bank only on high-concept or script-oriented comedies but are developing some dramas and thrillers as well—as long as they meet the concerns just stated. Let's look at their past winning releases and then move on to the up-and-coming projects.

• • • • • • • • • • • • • • •

PARENTHOOD

A big success for Imagine, this exemplifies how a film can get made as a result of the deal getting made—without a script. How to describe this in one line? Here's one way:

A funny "thirtysomething" with the theme that parenting never ends.

• • • • • • • • • • • • • •

THE BURBS

This is a comedy about paranoia in suburbia. The reviews were mixed. However, according to reported box office receipts of $40 million early in its distribution, the audiences went for it.

· · · · · · · · · · · · · · · ·

OPPORTUNITY KNOCKS

Imagine's development executive, David Friendly, recalls that he read the script on a Sunday and drove up to Brian Grazer's house immediately. And, by the way, it's generally thought throughout the industry that if something is liked you'll hear about it right away. Unlike bad news, good news about a deal comes fast. At any rate, the story elements that were liked run along these lines:

> **A small-time scamster breaks into a house, intent on robbing it. He hears on the answering machine that the housesitter—an uppercrust MBA—isn't able to come and fulfill his promise to watch the place while the owners are away. So the burglar comes back and housesits, impersonating the MBA. He inadvertently falls in love with the owner's daughter.**

More succinctly, this movie is a *Trading Places* in the suburbs. Like its precursor, it deals with the question of heredity versus environment. After David Friendly got it to the rest of the decision makers, Imagine purchased this script for $47,000 with a *blind commitment* for the writers to write their second screenplay for Imagine, regardless of whether it was the writers' idea or if it was to come from the company. There was an additional clause which provided that the writers would get a big fee if the movie got made. This is also known as "back end money." Obviously, with the movie long into its release, that has come to pass.

What may interest Hollywood snoops is that three other teams of writers were subsequently hired after the first-draft purchase. First came writers Lowell Ganz and Babaloo Mandel—known for doing *Splash*, *Parenthood*, and *Night Shift*. Next rewrite man was Henry Olek, who scripted *All of Me*. Finally, the writers of *Dream Team*, David Loucka and Jon Connolly, did the last rewrite. The director of *Mystic Pizza*—Donald Petrie—was brought on as director. By the time the final screenplay was done, the project had cost somewhere between $500,000 and $600,000. It began on an initial investment of $47,000.

• • • • • • • • • • • • • •

BACK DRAFT

With Ron Howard directing, this movie has the tag line "*Top Gun* in a firehouse."

It's about a fireman, naturally, and will be distributed by Universal.

• • • • • • • • • • • • • •

KINDERGARTEN COP

This came in as a pitch by Murray Salem, who is represented by agent David Wardlow. The story points and details about the project are compelling:

> **A burned-out Boston cop (Arnold Schwarzenegger) has lost his son. He must catch a dangerous criminal by teaching kindergarten, since he needs to get some information from a child in the class. The kindergarten kids change the cop's life, and in the end he decides to become a teacher.**

• • • • • • • • • • • • • •

Of course, by knowing what precedents exist within a given company, you wouldn't want to pitch them something exactly like what they're already doing. You would want to match their choices of genre, tone, style, and general thematic concerns.

There are certain precedents in the industry based on negative experiences with specific genres. An unforgettable and unfortunate example was *Heaven's Gate*. Although a western hadn't really worked since *Butch Cassidy and the Sundance Kid*, the studio gave the go-ahead to a western which never in their wildest dreams should have cost what it did. This was a situation of moviemaking that got out of hand and one that reminded everyone in the business to look for recent success-ful precedents in any genre.

HEROES AND HEROINES

One of the most familiar formulas that seems to exist in every genre is the use of the classic hero. Hollywood always loves a hero. Some of the best known and most beloved heroes and heroines are found in *Witness*, *Norma Rae*, and the *Rocky*, *Star Wars*, and *Indiana Jones* movies. Simply put, a hero makes the hard choice and does the right thing. A heroic protagonist is put into a situation of jeopardy and through a series of tests, against the odds, does the right thing and wins.

Chris Vogler is a teacher at UCLA's extension program and a veteran Hollywood story analyst who has been kind enough to let us discuss some of his work in regard to heroes and heroines as found in mythic structures. Many of Vogler's ideas are attributed directly to Joseph Campbell, particularly to Campbell's *The Hero with a Thousand Faces*. In the course of evaluating over five thousand screenplays, Vogler has found immeasurable help from an outline he has developed based on Campbell's examination of every hero's journey. In fact, many studio executives have urged their story departments to familiarize themselves with the same steps of every pro-tagonist's journey as those we are about to explore:

ACT I

STEP 1—THE ORDINARY WORLD

Show your protagonist in the everyday world—which will contrast with the strange new world he will soon be entering. The quintessential example is *The Wizard of Oz*, in which we see Dorothy in her everyday Kansas existence just before her journey begins. As Chris Vogler points out, the black-and-white footage of Kansas dramatizes the contrast with the technicolor world Dorothy will soon enter.

STEP 2—THE CALL TO ADVENTURE

The hero is presented with a problem or challenge that will change his destiny. It sets up and demands that he attain a specific goal. While you should create powerful reasons why the hero must heed the call as happens in the original hero myths, you should also allow for plausible reasons why the hero might not make this difficult choice.

In an action/adventure movie this call might be established when the hero decides to go after the bad guys; in a mystery/thriller when a detective takes on a case. In a romantic comedy the call of love is heard when boy meets girl. A goal will arise out of all these situations, often posed as a question. Dorothy's challenge as she takes off on her adventure to meet the Wizard of Oz comes from her quest to return home to Kansas.

STEP 3—THE RELUCTANT HERO

The hero experiences fear of the unknown or fear of outside forces. Here we observe that the hero hasn't completely committed to the mission or thought through the ramifications of what he is setting off to do. In classic dramatic structure, as seen in Sophocles' *Oedipus Rex*, a warning against undertaking the journey is sometimes voiced by soothsayers or seers.

Whether the fear is internal or provoked by real threats, these moments of second thoughts will be interrupted by extenuating circumstances that land the hero in a state of no return. Alternately, the hero may receive a nudge in the next stage.

STEP 4—THE WISE ONE

Usually a wise old man or woman, the mentor gives guidance and support to the hero. As Chris Vogler states, "The relationship between hero and mentor is one of the most common themes in mythology, and one of the richest in its symbolic value."

The bond can be viewed as one between parent and child, teacher and student, expert and novice, or between God and human beings. In whatever context this relationship appears, the purpose of the mentor is to assist the hero in his transition to the other world. The mentor may provide the hero with special tools or magical devices to take along on the journey, such as the ruby slippers given to Dorothy by Glinda the Good Witch of the North.

ACT II

STEP 5—INTO THE OTHER WORLD/THE FIRST THRESHOLD

The adventure gets going. This is the first time that the hero has fully made the decision to accept the challenge. In movie structure, this is often the turning point between Act I—the setup of the hero's decision to act—and Act II, which portrays the action itself. Visually, this transition into the other world is frequently enacted in terms of travel. A jet or rocket ship blasts off; car engines rev up and the squad peels out; a ship is launched. In *The Wizard of Oz* Dorothy leaves on foot to travel down the Yellow Brick Road.

When using the steps of the hero's journey to develop your story for pitching, you may find that the action is less important to plot out than the previous stages as described in the Act I section. Nevertheless, you'll want to envision some of the specifics that could happen next along the road.

STEP 6—TESTS, ALLIES, AND ENEMIES

New challenges arise as the hero learns the rules of the other world. Now that the action is underway, the protagonist encounters both favorable and unfavorable consequences of his decision to act. Many times the hero is able to glean information pertinent to this other world and to the adventure ahead in out-of-the-way gathering places, such as bars, Western saloons, or sinister inns stationed along the path.

In these venues, the hero may be introduced to secondary characters who will serve as allies or love interests. Likewise, he may meet or receive warnings and tests from his main antagonist or lesser enemies.

STEP 7—THE INMOST CAVE/THE SECOND THRESHOLD

The hero comes to a dangerous place—the headquarters of the villain or the arena in which he will find the object of his quest. This can also be the hero's moment of truth: He must confront the innermost fears that hold him back.

Chris Vogler cites Joseph Campbell in explaining that in mythology the "inmost cave" is frequently represented by the land of the dead. Orpheus, for example, was forced to travel to Hades to rescue his beloved. Whether the setting is actually a cave, a maze, a labyrinth, or even a crazed car chase, this is an opportunity for the hero to acknowledge his mortality.

STEP 8—THE SUPREME ORDEAL

The hero hits rock bottom, is brought to the brink of death, and all appears to be lost. In a love story it is here that boy loses girl. At this step, the hero must seem to die so that he can be born anew. This is a life-or-death moment and often marks what Vogler sees as the second part of Act II.

The Supreme Ordeal may indeed be the appearance of what the hero realized he feared most. It is a pivotal plot point for audiences to be made to think that the hero might be dead so that they can rejoice when he is revived.

STEP 9—SEIZING THE SWORD

Having barely survived, the hero may now take possession of the prize he has been seeking. In a romantic comedy, this is where boy finally gets girl . . . at least for a love scene.

The acquisition of the sword (or whatever the object of the quest) doesn't mean that the journey has ended yet, however. Now the hero must apply his new wisdom or power before he can travel back to safety. Dorothy, for example, seizes the broomstick from the Wicked Witch, but must still present it to the Wizard before she can go home.

STEP 10—THE ROAD BACK

The hero deals with the consequences of having seized his prize. In action/adventure films adversaries spring into action, chasing the hero who has captured the goods. Forces hostile to the hero must be confronted, along with the ways that the hero's taking of the sword or elixir might have disturbed the order of this other world.

It is at this stage that the hero will proclaim his desire or need to bring the journey to an end and return to the ordinary world.

ACT III

STEP 11—RESURRECTION

A second life-or-death moment, when evil forces are given one last shot before being defeated. Transformed, the hero will triumph here again before returning to ordinary life changed by some new insight.

STEP 12—RETURN WITH THE ELIXIR

The hero, as he returns to the ordinary world, must bring back some token of his journey—a prize or lesson—or he is doomed to repeat his dangerous adventure. Dorothy has learned that "there's no place like home" and she has realized her own strengths in overcoming adversity along the way.

Because of his possession of the elixir, the ordinary world as the hero once knew it has been changed by his new knowledge. This motif of coming full circle has been played out in a wide array of myths, literature, and films. Movie directors often heighten our awareness of the changed world by staging similar—yet still different—opening and closing shots.

I offer the above outline as a tool for you to either use in working on a screenplay based on your own idea or for you to see how your idea might be developed beyond its core concept and subject matter. If, for instance, we trace the steps taken in *Star Wars*, we find how well it adheres to the heroic formula and why this story structure has so much appeal. The Call to Adventure for Luke Skywalker is the mission to rescue Princess Leia. The Wise One, the mentor, of course, comes with the appearance of Obi-Wan Kenobi. The Inmost Cave comes at the point where Luke is sucked into the Death Star; the Supreme Ordeal stage happens when Luke is drawn into the trash-maker, with the audience wondering whether he is dead or alive. The Road Back is the exciting chase sequence wherein Luke and the Princess escape their pursuers through space. In his Resurrection and Return—through the final battle—Luke takes command over "the Force."

Numerous classic novels and films have employed the foregoing formula with great success, each with enough variations to allow for the story to become unique. So, if you are planning the steps of your hero's journey, you needn't be rigid about working with this tool; use your creativity and individuality in the process. Chris Vogler also cautions against blatantly throwing mythological terminology into a pitch. Stating, for example, that your hero goes through a "supreme ordeal" and then "returns with the elixir" may lead to an executive's reaction of "Huh?"

While it's true that not all movies use the heroic motif, do note that your characters will always be judged as to whether or not they are sympathetic and whether or not they undergo a transformation. The rationale is that the average moviegoer wants to identify with the lead and can be put off by certain extreme personality traits. For this reason, it's wise to avoid making your main character an alcoholic or drug addict, mentally unstable or just plain nuts, or someone with supernatural powers. Also, since many stars are wary about showing themselves in an unsympathetic light, your lead will be hard to cast—unless he or she undergoes some kind of important individual growth. On the other side of the spectrum, make sure your protagonist is fleshed out enough to be believable, complex enough for an actor to want the role.

Just how much of the plot you really need before pitching your idea is a question that doesn't always have a concrete answer. Sometimes you can go into a meeting and preface the pitch by saying that you haven't worked out the whole story, but you want to try out what you think is a really great high-concept idea. Your tag or one-liner may spark so much interest that the executive will help to fill in the blanks as far as subject matter or plot is concerned. In other cases, you may give your brief rundown of the idea and then be asked if you've thought through the story yet. For that reason, it's always best to be prepared and at least to be able to discuss the general beats of your story.

The beginning of a story is where the action really starts, where a mission is proclaimed, where a question is stated. The middle covers the resulting complications up to a crisis point. The end is how it all turns out. One way to sharpen your skills in this area is to look at fairy tales or simple, well-known fables and observe these three phases of the story. As we'll see in the subsequent examples, age-old fairy tales have long been the stuff from which movies have been made.

•••••••••••••

CINDERELLA

The Beginning: In private, poor but beautiful Cinderella wishes that she, like her mean and ugly stepsisters, could go to the Prince's ball. Her fairy godmother appears and grants her wish with one stipulation: Be gone by midnight.

The Middle: A major hit with the Prince at the ball, Cinderella almost forgets the warning and escapes just in the nick of time, accidentally leaving her tiny glass slipper behind.

The End: Having combed the kingdom looking for the woman whose foot fits the slipper, the Prince finally overcomes the interference of the mean and ugly stepsisters and finds Cinderella. They live happily ever after.

Cinderella stories and rags-to-riches plots are always popular.

•••••••••••••

BEAUTY AND THE BEAST

The Beginning: Because of a debt owed to the Beast by Beauty's father, Beauty is forced to live with the Beast. (This is comparable, by the way, to what is known in screenwriting as a "ghost," or an event that has happened before the story starts.)

The Middle: Although the Beast has been kind to Beauty, she is homesick for her family and he permits her to return for a brief visit. When she doesn't come back at the appointed time, the Beast is so broken-hearted that he falls into a near-death state.

The End: Having heard the sad news, Beauty rushes to the Beast's side and agrees to marry him. Because of her true love, Beauty lifts the wicked curse that has caused him to be a Beast and he turns into the dashing prince he once was. They live happily ever after.

The theme that love conquers all has been used along these lines in numerous films, and this particular tale spawned a TV series of the same name.

················

HANSEL AND GRETEL

The Beginning: An impoverished woodsman can no longer care for his children, Hansel and Gretel, and abandons them in the woods.

The Middle: A witch who lives in an inviting ginger-bread cottage lures the children inside with plans to cook and eat them.

The End: At the last moment Gretel pushes the witch into the oven instead and the two children, now in possession of the witch's valuables, are able to reunite with their father.

One of the classic fairy tales reputedly told to keep children from wandering too far into the woods, this form has grown up into today's horror films.

················

THE UGLY DUCKLING

The Beginning: Upset from being constantly mocked by family members and other ducks in the group, the ugly duckling leaves its home in search of friends.

The Middle: The ugly duckling is very confused when he finds some new friends who not only treat him nicely but rave about his good looks.

The End: As he grows up with this new family, he finds out that he is, in fact, not a duck but a swan—the most admired and beautiful of all the birds.

Also known as a coming-of-age story, many a film has

followed the growth of an individual to the discovery of inner self-worth.

· · · · · · · · · · · · · · · ·

It may surprise you that while the fairy tale form appears to be overly simplistic, your description of a beginning, middle, and end of your movie concept needn't be much more elaborate. After you try your hand analyzing a few stories familiar to you, try doing the same thing with classic films. Take a look at any of the movies made by Alfred Hitchcock, Frank Capra, or John Ford (all different genres) and you should be able to pinpoint the three major beats of the story. Then see if you can verbalize those three phrases with a few sentences per act.

I can tell you in advance that when it's time for the studio to decide whether they want to buy your idea or not, its plot is going to be even more important than character growth. By explaining how the protagonist goes from point A to point B to point C, you will generally show the kind of character the protagonist is anyway. If your character is wonderfully appealing or dashing, that's great. But characters do not sell in the pitch meeting. Premises sell.

Everything we've been talking about so far—developing high-concept ideas, choosing genres and arenas, shaping characters and story formats—can make the difference in a movie's success. So let's review some box-office records to see how the ingredients mix together best.

THE BLOCKBUSTERS

From a September 1990 listing of the top fifty highest grossing films of all time (which incidentally includes the 1939 epic *Gone With the Wind* at number four and the 1956 *Ten Commandments* at number nine), let's now analyze the top ten movies on the list that were made after 1970.

#1 E.T. (1982)

A classic example of a fish-out-of-water story in which an alien is trying to get home. It plays upon the age-old proverb that "there's no place like home," as does the classic *Wizard of Oz*. When *E.T.* was first released, critics compared its impact on audiences to that of a classic fairy tale. Many children have a fantasy of a secret, imaginary playmate whom only the child can see or hear, that special best friend who can be confided in.

#2 STAR WARS (1977)

As we saw previously, this is a hero's tale done as an updated western with high-tech hardware and space-age special effects.

#3 JAWS (1975)

A classic horror film updated. It preys upon our most primal fears of being stranded in the ocean—no matter where you swim you aren't going to go any considerable distance. Couple that isolation with a monster whose teeth can kill or dismember you. This movie proves how well the *simple* concept—a man-eating shark—can succeed. It was based on a best-selling novel.

#4 RAIDERS OF THE LOST ARK (1981)

Steven Spielberg's homage to the kind of movie he used to watch as a kid—all of the Saturday matinee action/adventure reels shown before the main attraction. Knowing that today's audiences wouldn't stand for a "to be continued" short, Spielberg crammed as much action, suspense, and cliffhangers as possible into a two-hour movie; he enhanced it with special effects and a big budget.

#5 THE EMPIRE STRIKES BACK (1980)

A continuation of the hero myth.

#6 RETURN OF THE JEDI (1983)
More continuation of the hero myth.

#7 THE GODFATHER (1972)
The story here is a soap opera about a Mafia family. We get to be voyeurs into an always fascinating world—the Mafia—as we view the inner workings of everyday life in the underworld. Based on a best-selling novel, it already had a massive audience.

#8 THE STING (1973)
A buddy picture with action, comedy, and superstars in a period setting.

#9 THE EXORCIST (1973)
A contemporary horror film based on a bestseller. Not only does the devil take over the body of a little girl, but she too becomes frighteningly powerful. The impact is rooted in our primal fears about evil and its indiscriminate scourge as it terrorizes innocent victims.

#10 SATURDAY NIGHT FEVER (1977)
A musical with dancing and a love story that took excellent advantage of the 1970s disco craze.

The films on the next list hover high in gross receipts when assessed for box-office revenues combined with video sales and rentals. These should also give you some insight into the makings of a box-office smash.

BEVERLY HILLS COP (1984)
A fish-out-of-water story as well as a buddy picture. It pairs a cop from the seedy world of Detroit with the upscale Beverly Hills police force.

GHOSTBUSTERS (1984)

Here's a comedy/fantasy that is bigger than life. Remember the tag line: "They're Here to Save the World." The structure is just that—it's the throughline done with megastars and special effects.

GREASE (1978)

Based on a Broadway musical, the movie was released to a market turned on by the existence of its already enormously successful soundtrack album. The presence of a huge star, John Travolta, also helped.

BATMAN (1989)

Based on a comic book hero—added to a big budget, a stylish look, and major stars.

BACK TO THE FUTURE (1985)

Another comedy/fantasy with a clever, simple science fiction gimmick along with special effects. It taps a basic human desire: to go back and change the past, replacing it with what you wish had happened.

TOOTSIE (1982)

Classic high-concept here: a man dressing up like a woman. It's always funny. The other asset: Dustin Hoffman. He dresses up like a woman in order to get a job; in so doing he becomes a better man.

CLOSE ENCOUNTERS OF THE THIRD KIND (1977)

Spielberg took this science fiction phrase and explored on screen what a close encounter would mean for a normal American family. It asks a universally pondered question: "Are we alone in the cosmos?"

INDIANA JONES AND THE TEMPLE OF DOOM (1984)
The Saturday matinee cliffhangers live on.

SUPERMAN (1978)
Like the more recent megahit *Batman*, this film derives from the love of comic book heroes who have been around for fifty years.

Aside from those films that have gained status as the all-time blockbusters, there were some big money makers during individual years prior to 1989. Let's examine them.

THREE MEN AND A BABY (1988)
A fish-out-of-water story done to the third degree. Instead of one fish, three bachelors are suddenly forced to act in the mode of the traditional housewife, thus entering the world of child-raising. This is also *Mr. Mom* times three.

BIG (1988)
Definitely high-concept. It illustrates how to shape ideas from a "what if" question. What if a little boy made a wish to be big . . . and his wish came true?

FATAL ATTRACTION (1987)
An urban thriller that touches everyone who is married or in a relationship and has ever wondered about the risks of having an affair. Taking that commonplace possibility and exaggerating it to the nth degree, this then becomes your worst nightmare—the seemingly normal person with whom you have an affair turns out to be psychotic. The lives of your most cherished family members are threatened; your whole existence is shattered.

Some critics who viewed this movie from a sociological perspective have suggested that it paralleled the emergence

of new consciousness about the need to be sexually mono-
gamous. The film illustrates how plugging into timely concerns can underscore box office success.

FERRIS BUELLER'S DAY OFF (1987)

This shows John Hughes's wonderful facility for simple
ideas that appeal to a youth market. What is an everyday
wish for kids between the ages of ten and twenty-one? If
they're in school, one of the most common desires is to play
hooky. The story then covers one boy's experiences as he
follows through on his wish.

CROCODILE DUNDEE (1986)

A fish-out-of-water comedy in which a backwoodsman
from Australia enters the urban world of New York City.

WITNESS (1985)

In passing, we saw that this film employs the structure of
the hero's journey. This murder mystery also has elements
of a dramatic love story and to some degree that of the fish-
out-of-water story. As a foreigner plunged into the unique
world of the Amish, Harrison Ford's character must ultimately return to his own world. You can get excellent insight
from such a film as to what you can do with subject matter
or arenas gleaned from reference guides. The ways of the
Amish, in this instance, offer compelling details not generally known to the average moviegoer.

NATIONAL LAMPOON'S EUROPEAN VACATION (1985)

The film follows the same principle spotted in *Ferris Buel-
ler's Day Off*. Almost everyone has been on a summer vacation and we all know that excursions taken with the family
can either turn into tragedy or comedy. What about a combination—a comic nightmare in which funny mishaps turn
into hilarious disasters? The makers of this movie gambled
on the thinnest of concepts, but the movie was a big success.

The subject—the old "What I did on my summer vacation"—might seem overly mundane and thin. But it works because it is so accessible. Who can't relate to it? And subjects like it will also work for you, as long as they haven't already been overdone.

Let's move forward in time again and look now at the nine highest ranking films at the box office during the summer of 1989 and count the number of those based on original ideas.

1. *Indiana Jones—The Last Crusade:* a sequel to a film based on a genre
2. *Batman:* based on a comic book hero
3. *Dead Poets Society:* an original idea
4. *Ghostbusters II:* a sequel to a film from an original idea
5. *Field of Dreams:* based on a book
6. *Beaches:* based on a book
7. *No Holds Barred:* an idea as star vehicle for Hulk Hogan
8. *Do the Right Thing:* an original idea
9. *K–9:* an original idea; pure high-concept

Out of those nine top movies, we have a total of five original ideas. Chalk up another victory for idea power.

THE BOTTOM LINE

As you juggle these various ingredients to see how marketable your idea is going to be, you'll begin to decide how much you personally want to emphasize high concept. You've probably concluded by now that a strong, simple high-concept idea can be a star vehicle unto itself. Besides having a built-in publicity campaign in their very wording, those one-liners, too, will show you off to your best advantage when you are ready to pitch.

To establish *your* bottom line in the marketability of *your* ideas, learn to play your hunches, to fine-tune your commercial instincts as a consumer. Try to be objective about your idea, separating yourself from it and asking this question: Would you and your peers pay money to see it as a movie? My hunch is that if you can answer yes, then you've got yourself an idea that can become a commercial property.

CHAPTER 6
FACT AND FICTION

"I find that the hardest thing to develop in my students is some kind of narrative vigor. We have lost the capacity to tell stories. We no longer believe in make-believe. I think most of us at heart, intellectually, are documentarians. We observe reality, and we try to reproduce our observations."

—Critic and author Andrew Sarris on writing for films, from an interview in *Movie People*, edited by Fred Baker with Ross Firestone

Reality is far too expansive a realm to be defined or debated here, but it should be noted that there is a special movie reality that can be described as being larger than life. Not to be confused in this sense with cinéma vérité, which is a particular style of filmmaking, movie reality differs from TV reality; both differ—as shown in the quote above—from journalistic and documentary reality. In culling ideas from real life, it often becomes difficult to know how much fact and how much fiction will give your idea that movie reality —or a TV reality, for that matter. There are also legal constraints to be addressed when pitching ideas which are mostly based in fact. Furthermore, when your idea is taken from another person's true story, you'll want to know the optimal ways to partner with that person. In many cases, as a creative idea person, you will choose whether to fictionalize the story or to develop it as a nonfiction project.

We'll start by looking at what to do when someone says "Have I got a story for you":

PRICK UP YOUR EARS

In the not too distant past, I was having Thanksgiving dinner and was seated next to a cousin who happens to be a well-respected doctor in Los Angeles. Knowing I worked in the movie world, my cousin mentioned that he had a funny story idea based on rumors about some shady dealings in the medical world—did I want to hear it? Of course, this happens all the time and chances are that just anyone's funny story idea probably won't be substantial enough for a movie. But, as the rule goes—you never know. So I gave it a listen and threw in a couple suggestions:

. . . .

Suppose a doctor performs surgery on a woman and she subsequently sues the insurance company for $10 million over a grievance having to do with the surgery. And later it is revealed that the surgeon and the woman are in cahoots in order to scam the insurance company. In the end, a huge medical sting is uncovered which no one saw coming.

. . . .

I told my cousin that it was a good idea and, if he would agree, I'd write up a one-page outline and try pitching it. Indeed, it was sold and made as a TV movie called "The Operation," which starred Joe Penny. Imagine my ob-gyn cousin's delight when his "funny story," plucked and fictionalized from the real world of medicine, was aired on CBS. Additionally, I was given a producing credit and he received story credit. He received story money and technical consultant salary. It happened because he had the wherewithal to

bring the story up and because I was able to see it as potentially bigger than life.

In the event that you don't find people tossing good ideas
on your plate, try the next ploy:

CONDUCT A TALK SHOW

No, I don't necessarily mean as in a cable-run talk show, but
more the kind you host in your own living room. One time,
almost inadvertently, while having dinner with an old
friend, Jeff Silverman, I found myself accidentally conduct-
ing an informal interview. Per a TV interviewer's style, I
asked Jeff what was the most interesting thing that ever happened to him in college. His response at first was sort of a
"funny you should ask," but here was Jeff's true story:

• •

Back in the late sixties, Jeff was attending a men's school
when he heard that Vassar was opening its doors to men for
the first time. An all-woman school was going co-ed and Jeff
became one of the first males to go to Vassar. What a shock
to his parents, who hoped to call him "our son, the doctor."
Now it was to be "our son, the daughter." What a culture
shock—a fish-out-of-water experience—for Jeff, when suddenly he was surrounded by a thousand young women.

• •

And now, Jeff Silverman's true story is called "All Good
Men" and was sold to Tri-Star Pictures. How did that come
to pass? Well, even though I did some checking and was told
by everyone that they'd heard the idea of boys going to girls'
schools before, I came up with a way to support the idea.
With the help of a producing partner, William Blaylock, I got
it to a star—Michael J. Fox—who liked the idea and wanted
to play the part. Then, when I came walking into a studio

with Michael J. Fox, nobody said that they had already heard the idea before!

Through these two fortunate episodes, you can understand why I firmly believe that everyone has a story to tell. Because of the inherent value in a real-life situation, I urge you to:

DO THE LEGWORK

When you come across an idea from a newspaper or magazine article, from a radio or TV news show, a good deal of work is sometimes required. You have to research the subject area. You may have to track down the person, establish whether you need to option the rights to a story, and in that event option or buy the rights. When a story that you didn't pursue winds up being done, you'll be sorry that you didn't try harder. And when a story that you didn't acquire ethically and legally gets produced, you may find yourself in a real mess.

Researching a subject area can yield enough information that you may be able to sell your idea without getting rights from an individual. Suppose, for example, you read an article about a new group of teenage environmentalists and your research turns up the fact that there are lots of these groups. In that case you don't have to track them all down.

As far as the tracking is concerned, use commonsense skills. Make phone calls to the sources where you saw or heard the story; be forthright about why you want to be in touch with the person and you'll usually get plenty of help.

We will begin by looking at someone else's real-life experience that probably altered my Hollywood destiny more than any other project. To give you a taste of the excitement I felt as each leg of the journey was reached, I take you back to 1975, where you'll find me in New York in the following straits:

PHASE ONE—TRAPPED IN ROCKEFELLER CENTER

How had this come to pass? Well, for starters, I'd obtained a wonderful opportunity working for producer Gil Shiva. At the time, European director Lina Wertmuller had captured the sensibilities of American audiences with tour de force films such as *Seven Beauties* and *Swept Away*. Subsequently, Gil had struck a fortunate partnership with Lina Wertmuller and the two of them, as a producer/director team, had been given a deal by Warner Brothers to make Ms. Wertmuller's first American film. What's more, Warner Brothers had signed them for a three-picture deal. It was quite a coup for all parties and was heralded in all the trade papers as an unprecedented union of domestic and international filmmaking.

After meeting me in California, Gil offered me a job that would entail finding new scripts for Ms. Wertmuller. So off I'd gone to New York along with the notion that I might eventually co-produce one of the films. I had moved from script reader to producer's assistant and I thought I was ready for anything.

Our office was located at 75 Rockefeller Center and my days were filled with reading all the new scripts that were literally pouring in. Every screenwriter in the world, it seemed, wanted Lina Wertmuller to direct his or her movie. Very soon, however, it became clear that Lina was intent on doing her own movie. In fact, her most heartfelt choice was a twelve-hundred-page draft of "Caligula." The studio immediately rejected it. In a compromise, she opted to do a film called "A Night Full of Rain," based on a script she then wrote.

In due time, the start date was set to shoot this movie, which was to star Candice Bergen and Giancarlo Giannini. Off Gil Shiva went to Italy, joining Wertmuller et al as production got under way. I found myself, at this juncture, continuing to read scripts for the planned follow-up films. And yet, practically alone in the big Warner Brothers office, I also found myself feeling somewhat removed from the more compelling elements of film production.

Feeling a bit trapped, I decided to make use of the extra hours.

PHASE TWO—THE SEARCH FOR FUTURE PROJECTS

While still keeping my eye out for potential Wertmuller scripts, I began to explore ideas, stories, and screenplays that I might pursue at a later date.

Left to my own devices, I used many of the techniques presented in our previous look at where ideas are found. The newspaper (in this case the *New York Times*) was to be my first gold mine. On a quiet Saturday afternoon, while browsing through the sports section, I noticed a short article on the next to last page.

The story told of a boy named Pat Lajko who'd done an unusual thing. In less than ten brief paragraphs, the newspaper article struck me as containing a perfect movie idea.

PHASE THREE—A GOOD IDEA

While this syndicated UPI piece focused on the illegality of Lajko's actions, what truly interested me was that Peter Pan real-life experience of someone who didn't want to grow up. After lettering in college gymnastics at Iowa State University, twenty-four-year-old Patrick Lajko donned the false identity of Scott Johnson and enrolled himself in East High School, located in Wichita, Kansas.

For a year, Scott Johnson, a.k.a. Pat Lajko, led East High's gymnastics team to overwhelming success and his own reputation as a star athlete continued to grow. Only after an anonymous tip to authorities was Pat Lajko's cover blown. Also implicated in the scam were three others, including a student aide who had assisted Pat in forging his high school transcript. Officials fingered Pat Lajko after stopping the bus that was taking the team to a swim meet. Although Pat's charade was over, he said he didn't regret a second of his incredible adventure.

I knew by the mere fact that a newspaper writer had seen fit to do the story that it was newsworthy. I could only hope, somewhere down the line, that someone in the industry—besides me—might find it to be "studioworthy." But, familiar as I was with commercial concepts, I was certain that this offbeat, out-of-the-ordinary true experience was at least a good contender.

In addition to Lajko's story being true, it asked an age-old question: What would you do if you could go back to a period in your life and re-create it as you would have wanted it to be? Many films based on such a universal desire have been produced, though they usually employ some form of magic or science fiction. Devils or angels or fairy godmothers are first required to work their hocus-pocus or supernatural powers before the human protagonist can follow through on the desire. In *Damn Yankees*, as one example, an older man was given the chance to go back and become a baseball player via the guidance of Satan. In *It's a Wonderful Life*, the main character meets a guardian angel, who shows him what the world would have looked like if he'd never lived. In the case of *Back to the Future*, the transportation to the past was provided by the fantastic time-traveling capabilities of a De Lorean car.

So my enthusiasm, as you can imagine, was escalating when I considered that this young man had time traveled without the assistance of fantasy. I knew at once that I had to meet this guy.

PHASE FOUR—TRACKING THE SOURCE

Having no experience acquiring rights to true stories, I did what came naturally and called the *New York Times*. I then made another series of phone calls to UPI, to a Wichita paper, to several reporters in the interim, to the actual author of the article, and to Pat Lajko's parents. I finally got the real McCoy on the wire.

I introduced myself and explained that I was interested in discussing his story as a possible movie project. I asked him whether he would be willing to fly to New York to meet with me. Without hesitating, Pat jumped at the offer and admitted that he'd never been out of the Midwest. He was thrilled with my interest, while I was moderately surprised that no one else had yet contacted him.

Let me interject an important point. Very often, when stumbling upon what you think is a great idea, you'll automatically assume that thousands of other people are scrambling to buy the rights and that you don't stand a chance. The reality is that something which strikes your fancy may have gone unnoticed by others.

I had to beg, borrow, and plead from among friends and family, but as soon as I could, I sent Pat the airplane ticket and, a few days later, dashed off to meet his plane. My investment also included putting him up at the New York Hilton for two nights, in addition to providing meals and transportation.

After getting him checked in, we went on to have a story meeting, New York style, over dinner. Hearing more details from this extremely likable young man, I was even more convinced that a terrific movie was about to be born. At the end of our second meeting, I finally got around to explaining that I wanted to buy the rights to his story. To that end, I told him I would be sending him a legal agreement, drawn up by a lawyer, and if it met with his approval we would have a deal.

Pat Lajko was so enthralled by the circumstances that he spent another day sightseeing in New York. Meanwhile, I looked around for an inexpensive yet competent lawyer. (An impossible dream.)

PHASE FIVE—ACQUIRING THE RIGHTS

Determined as I was, I found a friend who had an entertainment lawyer and I paid to have a very simple legal agreement drawn up. It stipulated that I, Bob Kosberg, as producer, was going to give Pat Lajko $500 in return for his giving me an option on his life story. That option would last for a year and give me the authority to present his story to the various Hollywood studios. If I was successful in getting one of those entities to buy the story from me, then Pat Lajko would receive more money at the screenwriting stage as well as an opportunity to be hired as story consultant at the production stage. It was my plan to be a producer, or at least one of the producers, and I also left open the possibility of my being hired as the screenwriter.

My real-life character was so pleased with the agreement that he signed it and returned it to me immediately.

PHASE SIX—THE TIME FACTOR

Had things been different, I would have had trouble selling Pat's story. I only had one year and I was still working for Gil Shiva and Lina Wertmuller. But I realized Wertmuller's three-picture deal would most likely end after the first picture was released. So I went to Gil and explained that I wanted to head back to Hollywood to pursue my writing and producing career.

While Gil encouraged my choice, he likewise cautioned, "Be careful when you go back to Los Angeles, Robert. There are sharks out there and they'll eat you alive." As he uttered these ominous words, I was unfazed, thinking, "Oh, he's just being a conservative New York producer who doesn't trust anybody from Los Angeles." Paying little heed to his warning, I made haste to get back to Hollywood, where I instantly found myself in:

PHASE SEVEN—SWIMMING WITH THE SHARKS

Okay, so I wasn't eaten alive, but I was certainly nibbled at. . . .

Nevertheless, I had some ammunition: my trusty newspaper article and what I figured was an excellent title for the movie idea I wanted to sell. I'd opted to dub the story "Back Flip"—a comedy about a gymnast who does a back flip from college to high school. I'd also come up with a way to pitch the project, which was to concentrate on how this true tale embodied the Peter Pan fantasy lurking in just about everyone. Leaving the zone of hard fact, the time had come to add more fiction. The hero, as I saw him, didn't want to ever grow up. He felt a need to go back to his past and make it better, to live out his dreams of how he wished high school could have been. The comic elements were all there, not only in his disguise but in how various complications would arise when some of his efforts—dating the cutest cheerleader, winning all the awards—would fail.

Some of the Hollywood "sharks" began to circle. It wasn't until Marty Caan, an agent at William Morris, took a shine to the idea that things began to move forward. Impressed that I had the article and the rights, Caan introduced me to his clients Bob Christianson and Rick Rosenberg, a producing team. At that time, these two were primarily known for producing television movies and were looking to segue into producing feature films. "Back Flip" appealed to them and they thought they could set it up at a studio. With Marty Caan's assistance as well, the project was presented to United Artists, headed then by Mike Medavoy. Luckily, the article intrigued the pertinent players at United Artists and finally Mike Medavoy put "Back Flip" into development.

It had taken me less than thirty days since my return to Hollywood to sell my first project as a producer. United Artists gave me $5,000 to acquire the rights to the story, and when I totaled up the expenses of my initial investment on the deal (including the twenty-five cents for the *New York Times*) I saw that I had more than five times my money back. I was beginning to like being a producer.

PHASE EIGHT—ONLY THE BEGINNING

Not wanting to jeopardize my first Hollywood deal, I did not insist that I be hired as the screenwriter for Pat Lajko's story. For that role, Christianson and Rosenberg hired a writer by the name of Alan Swyer. He and I met at the legendary Hollywood restaurant, Musso and Frank's, for my first producer's story meeting with a writer. We talked about how we both saw the story, and a few months down the line the script was delivered. Unfortunately, United Artists did not see fit to continue development or, as would have been preferable, to go ahead and make the movie. "Back Flip" was put into turnaround, a limbo state we will define more precisely later on.

I was justifiably disappointed, but at the same time I learned an equally valuable lesson. One moment I was selling a project to a studio and looking at a contract that said I was going to be a producer, making upward of a hundred thousand dollars *if* the movie was made. In what seemed like the very next moment, that dream was over. That is how fast the game is played. Rather than feeling discouraged, I was happy that my pursuits thus far had gotten me an agent at William Morris and provided me with access to the industry. I knew that my next move was to do the same thing all over again. And again and again, until finally something would hit and get made. Fortunately, it took me one more try with a real-life story to achieve that goal.

Using all the tactics I'd learned from my first go-around with "Back Flip," my partner, David Simon, and I had little trouble tracking down Sonny Wisecarver in Las Vegas. This was the fellow who had come into national renown in the forties as the "Woo-woo Kid."

Although we've mentioned the deal-making aspects of this project, it may be interesting to note that the article about Sonny Wisecarver came from one of those "Where are they now?" columns which appear in many newspapers. I saw the blurb about Elsworth "Sonny" Wisecarver in the *Los Angeles Times*, but before I was really hooked on the idea, I did extensive research about his famed past in the UCLA library's periodical reference section. Sure enough, several different magazines and newspapers dating back to the mid-forties had picked up on this young Romeo's exploits. As a mere fifteen-year-old, Sonny survived a rough family life by engaging the romantic interests of the wives left alone by husbands then fighting in World War II. Tall and charming, he was apparently wonderful company for these women. Then he ran off with one of these "older" gals (she was twenty-five) and got married, despite the fact that he was underage. Even though that marriage was subsequently annulled, Sonny waited just long enough for the fervor to die down and then went off and did it again with a second woman.

The boy became known as "Oh what a man Wisecarver," a latter-day Lothario. My parents remembered him and also recalled that Bob Hope, at the time, was doing Sonny Wisecarver jokes; singers on the Sunset Strip were writing songs about him. While his legendary status didn't last forever, Sonny indeed had what Andy Warhol called his "fifteen minutes of fame."

By 1976, when I first read the article, Sonny was living in Las Vegas and that's where we found him. Now all David and I had to do was somehow convince Sonny to sell us his rights. It turned out that several parties over the years had inquired about the possibility of optioning his story. Why he agreed to sell the rights to us, as opposed to others who reputedly offered more initial option money, probably had to do with the fact that he believed we would do justice in our presentation of his experiences. This is a very subtle point that underscores yet again just how much enthusiasm sells.

THE PRICE YOU PAY

One dollar. That's right, for one dollar you can option the rights to someone's true story. You are neither exploiting nor ripping off the individual; you're inviting him or her to enter into a joint venture. The two of you are gambling together. For that dollar you are given the facts, and in return you must supply the fiction—the creativity and the vision to promote the story as larger than life. Aside from the ingenuity, you are contributing your business savvy—your expertise in pitching plus your ability to provide access . . . to get through the studio doors and pitch the story to a "buyer." You're gambling by taking a chance on the story and investing your time without pay to secure a deal. The other person is gambling that you can really deliver on your promise to sell and produce his or her story. Have an understanding— better yet, a written agreement—with your partner that for a prescribed amount of time (one month to one year) you are going to the studios and/or producers with the story and the deal between the two of you will be negotiated in good faith at the point interest is shown.

You may have a problem if the story is really hot and more than one producer has contacted the source. As a show of faith that they really believe in a story, some producers will pay large amounts of option money, ranging from $500 to $25,000. If, on the other hand, you can genuinely convey your integrity and dedication to seeing the story done well, you can often overcome this hurdle. To someone who is unfamiliar with Hollywood, it may be helpful to explain that you are not a studio with power to buy the story for great sums of money. Yet, you should point out, you are that liaison to those who do have purchasing power. And besides, there's nothing unusual about optioning rights in this fashion. Even completed scripts are optioned by small production companies for minimal sums.

A legal document, or a two-page deal memo, is always advisable to protect both parties. While you can't preset exact terms until you've actually got a bid, you can outline general expectations from the deal on both sides. If you are a writer, this is a time to decide whether your plan includes writing the screenplay once the story has been bought. Owning the rights to a true story often impresses the executives. You have proven to have real entrepreneurial skills and may be able to get the very difficult first-draft screenplay deal. The deal memo that you have also gives the executive an idea of how much it's going to cost to control the story. Entering that domain without written parameters puts you at a disadvantage. It means you only have the rights to negotiate—which leaves open the possibility that your real-life person is going to come back when negotiation begins and ask for a $500,000 advance and a Ferrari. It happens every now and then. And what happens next is that the studio executive looks at you like you are the one who's crazy and your whole deal crumbles.

When dealing with facts, true stories, and real events, there is such a hazy shade of gray covering what can be acquired without rights that you should either go to law school or opt for this easier choice:

GET LEGAL ADVICE

In this business, too many hair-raising, problematical lawsuits to mention have occurred when an assumption was made about legalities. Laws vary from state to state; published material deemed in the public domain has a different break-off year, depending on how long ago it was written. Sometimes, when the person whose story you'd like to option is deceased, you aren't required to get rights. Alternately, there may be a family or an estate with whom you must negotiate. So when in doubt, always consult with a lawyer.

As long as you have found out what legal restrictions apply, you can be entrepreneurial by doing added research along various lines. Some published works from before the 1920s, for instance, have come into the public domain. Some celebrities and real-life public figures are said to belong to the public domain, meaning you can sometimes use their names (not information about their private lives) in your story in the context of public events. Because of what is called the "Son of Sam" law, criminals cannot receive money in return for the rights to their stories; but permission to use material pertinent to a criminal still can be required. When there is more than one person involved in the true story, you can obtain rights from the key people and fictionalize the others. Just remember, anything that would place the studio in a position of being liable is going to be a liability for you. Let me reiterate, though: Even when you are not in doubt, check it out with a lawyer.

I'll add at this juncture that what's most appealing about a movie based on a true story isn't only that it's true. What's also appealing on the screen, and what will make it salesworthy, is your particular take on it. So, as you begin to visualize how you see this real-life event translating to a film, you may gain further insights by considering the medium of television—an area we have not discussed before.

TELEVISION

I don't have the necessary space in this book to cover all of the ins and outs of TV as I have done for feature films. However, all of the techniques we've discussed for finding movie ideas will work equally well when it comes to television. Television may not interest you as much as motion pictures do. Still, I'd like to point out that it is a major market for ideas as well as a great training ground for developing ideas. There are occasions when your idea may sell more readily as a TV movie than as a feature, so it should be helpful to explore some of the differences that exist between the two mediums.

One of the differences is that networks rarely negotiate a deal with a first-timer. Even with a good idea, you must usually first align yourself with an established production company, which can then walk you and your material into the networks. It's common knowledge that networks are very conservative and cautious. They definitely prefer to buy material from colleagues (referred to in television as "suppliers") with whom they deal on a daily basis.

Even if you bought the rights to a riveting true story and you were able to get some network interest, the network would probably require that you join up with their choice of production company to produce the story. As you can see, much more of a closed-door policy exists in televison than in features. Yet I still maintain that if you're someone with lots of ideas, you should definitely explore both markets.

When people come to me with ideas, for example, I explain that I'm primarily interested in feature films and TV movies. I'll sometimes consider ideas for television series and game shows. (However, other producers may be open to ideas for news shows, variety specials, talk shows, rock concerts, and documentaries.) A recurring question has been whether there is a discernible difference between a feature idea and a TV movie idea. Yes, there are—so let's describe some of them now.

How Explicit Is It?

Ideas like a *Robocop* or a *Lethal Weapon* have too much hard-edged action and too much violence for a TV movie. Likewise, *No Way Out* and *Jagged Edge* are too sexually explicit for television. Even explicit comedy—off-beat, wild, and bizarre humor—suggests unsafe ground for television. There are exceptions, such as the tone of Fox's "Married . . . with Children" or some shows being tried on pay TV and cable channels. But nine times out of ten, pitching explicit subject matter will get the response, "That could *never* be done for network television."

How Big Is the Budget?

The more expensive to film and the longer the time required to shoot the movie, the more apt it is to be considered a feature. TV movies are shot in a much shorter time period with a much lower budget.

Would It Attract Big Stars?

In some cases, a TV movie subject that attracted big-name actors has been elevated to the feature arena. A story such as *Kramer vs. Kramer* would immediately be seen as a TV movie —unless actors like Dustin Hoffman and Meryl Streep had committed to do it.

How Familiar Is It?

If you brought me the idea that a man murders his wife and then goes on the run to hide from the police, I'd tell you that you didn't have a feature idea. If your drug bust or murder stories could have been done on shows like "Miami Vice" or "Murder, She Wrote," put them in your TV file of ideas.

What Kind of Reality?

TV continues to like true-to-life stories. Those adventures that really happened seem to really interest the television networks. They are usually highly publicized stories or events, and network executives know that these kinds of movies will attract a sizable TV audience. Though ultimately the stories could fit just as well for either feature films or TV movies, they tend to sell most quickly to the networks. For various reasons, the type of true stories that deal with an individual trying to overcome a debilitating illness—referred to in the industry as "disease of the week" stories—have a better track record of selling to television.

Whenever I find an idea that is on the borderline between motion pictures and TV movies, I give it a shot at the studios first. If they all pass, then I proceed directly to the networks.

The type of movies which we've been referring to as bigger than life are those that the average moviegoer will pay $6 or $7 to see. Your feature idea should lend itself to that larger experience, to transporting the audience into another world, another reality.

But all of this is not to say that television ideas must only be reality-based. Like film, many different genres end up on TV. If you'd like to pursue a series idea, educate yourself by watching a wide scope of programming. Television has very discernible formulas that you can easily extract. By watching the TV movies as they air, you can obviously get a better idea of what the networks are looking for.

THE PUBLISHING ROUTE

Let's say, hypothetically, that you've read an article about a real person and you think the story contains movie potential. Let's suppose the individual spent many years searching for and then finally locating a sunken ship laden with treasure. And because you have been so entrepreneurial, you've managed to obtain the rights to the story. So far, so good.

Then, in gathering the details, you find that what makes the story so interesting is not the actual blow-by-blow account of how the treasure was found but more the individual and his philosophical discoveries while out at sea alone. Now, because philosophy does not make for an easy sell to Hollywood, you might consider developing this property first as a book. But before we get into the nitty-gritty of that process, let's first discuss some other reasons why a true event might lend itself better to book form before you attempt a movie pitch. Like most of the examples we'll soon mention, certain book-to-film leaps have been accomplished even when the story would originally have been shunned by studios.

The Action Occurs in the Mind

Stories of madness, like *Sybil* or even *Psycho*, are harder to present initially in movie terms. In a novel based on those true events or in a nonfiction book which documents the psychological changes, there will be much more freedom to depict a fascinating inner mental world.

Intellectual, philosophical, or spiritual discoveries can be made enthralling when artfully described in well-written narrative. Unfortunately, these matters can only be implied through the course of a movie's physical action.

Sexual Exploits

A true story that may be judged as pornographic (X-rated) by the movie industry may be explored more tastefully in a literary venue. Attitudes toward very sexy story lines do run in a cyclical manner in both Hollywood and New York's publishing world. As you might imagine, currrent trends show conservatism on the rise in both milieus. Nevertheless, I would venture a guess that a terrific true tale containing someone's sexual exploits will draw book-buying attention. Once the public has accepted the story in that area, studios will sometimes take the risk to develop the book as a movie. Usually, though, the film version will be less explicit. For example, the film *9½ Weeks* was based on the more graphic novel of the same name, which reputedly came from real life.

A Cast of Thousands

Factual stories that follow one person's experiences in connection with large groups of people or those that simply involve many characters are harder to track in a two-hour film rendering. Books based on true crime, like Truman Capote's *In Cold Blood*, or *The Choirboys* and others by Joseph Wambaugh, as well as expansive epics rooted in true war stories (Stephen Coonts's fictional *Flight of the Intruder*) give readers an easier way to meet and know all the various people who have played a part in the saga.

When your real-life person's experiences have included the participation of living famous persons, you may likewise find more enthusiastic buyers in the publishing world than in the film industry. Why this happens to be so can't be clearly gauged. What I can tell you is that if you are pitching, say, someone's behind-the-scenes love affair with a celebrity, many movie executives will advise you, "That's a book." Then, after the book has sold many thousands of copies, those same executives will assert, "That's a movie."

Marketing Strategy

Because, as we've seen, Hollywood is always more amenable to ideas proven marketable in a previous form, many writers and independent producers have elected to sell their projects first as books. Best-selling titles can then frequently be sold as films, often in what is known as a "bidding war," in which an agent or producer pits the studios against each other in a race to acquire the property. These, by the way, can be orchestrated for all different types of commercial projects—screenplays, packaged ideas, and books. With the book-into-movie sales of such titles as *Presumed Innocent* or *Rush*, a purchasing furor was created within the movie industry even before the books had been out in the bookstores long enough to attain best-selling status. In such instances, as much or more than a million dollars can be the going rate for the acquisition of movie rights.

Suppose you've managed to option the rights to someone's story which involves real-life harrowing espionage. Now you know, since you've seen books and movies dealing with this subject matter, that you could go in either direction

to put together a deal. What has been done in the past by
several marketing-minded individuals is to start the ball rolling by assembling a book package—you, the real-life person,
a credible writer, an agent, and a publisher. You can then
either wait for the book to start selling or you can immedi-
atley begin to entice studios to buy the rights.

Again, we can't cover the intricacies of the publishing business in the span of this book, but here is a brief outline of the
two steps you might pursue should you decide your project
has possibilities as a book:

STEP 1—PROPOSALS

To submit the story to a publisher, you will need to devise
a ten- to fifty-page proposal that covers a synopsis of story,
marketing, and promotional suggestions and usually at least
one sample chapter. If you are not a writer but simply the
person putting the project together, this is a good time to
bring in the skills of a qualified ghostwriter or co-author.

STEP 2—SUBMISSIONS

Not having an agent may pose a roadblock, as it does in
the process of submitting screenplays to Hollywood buyers.
Still, your proposal will sometimes be considered by a publisher with or without an agent representing it. The difference is the fact that agents have established relationships
with particular editors, which frequently accelerates the time
taken to read the proposal and improves the likelihood of a
sale. But, like Hollywood, publishers recognize a great story
and many books have been bought in this manner without
an attached agent. If there is interest in purchasing your
book idea, you should have no trouble finding an agent to
negotiate the terms.

For more information on the publishing route, continue in
an entrepreneurial vein by researching that field. The main
thing to remember is that if you have gone so far as to obtain

the rights to someone's true story or if you have a viable one of your own, you have gained a golden Hollywood opportunity.

As an ongoing study of the human condition, real-life stories have always been and will always continue to be sources of interest and inspiration. True accounts of modern-day heroes, villains, triumphs, and tragedies are universally appealing. Add to these true tales your own contributions of make-believe and good old American knowhow . . . and then you'll be ready to sell to Hollywood.

CHAPTER 7
PACKAGING YOUR IDEA

"... in movies, the answer to 'Who is a star?' is 'It's whoever *one* studio executive with 'go' power thinks is a star and will underwrite with a start date.' (A superstar is someone they'll *all* kill for. . . .)"

—William Goldman, from
Adventures in the Screen Trade

"**The director is both the least necessary and most important component in film-making.**"

—Andrew Sarris, from *The American Cinema*
—*Directors and Directions 1929–1968*

To whatever extent Goldman and Sarris are correct in their respective observations, the point to recognize is that attaching a star or a director to your project is going to give you a significant edge on your competition. From now until eternity, studios are going to have a backlog of projects "in development." So buying another idea that may add to the clutter isn't going to be anywhere near as appealing as taking on a project that is either a star vehicle or—better yet—already packaged.

The primary elements of a package are the property, the star or stars, the director, producer(s), and sometimes the writer(s). Before we get into the nitty-gritty of the packaging process, I should preface by saying I've got some bad news and some good news.

The bad news is that for people outside of Los Angeles and New York, it's almost impossible to package your own deal. Since all of the agents, managers, and production companies who represent the entities you need to contact are in L.A. or New York, you'll need to team up with a producer or an agent to be able to present your idea to those representatives. (Even if you reside in either of these two cities, you'll almost always need that agent or producer to be the liaison between you and the VIPs who could take on your project.)

Compounding the difficulty in packaging is the fact that even when you have an agent, that agent is up against other packaging agencies who want to package their deals in-house. *In-house* means that if the packaging agency can get a property sold and know that its key elements are all represented by the agency, the agency stands to benefit enormously. While you'd probably prefer to be represented by the agencies who can package in-house, these are the least accessible to individuals in the early stages of their careers. It's that old catch-22 again.

And now for the good news. Well, it's tied in to the major theme of this book, which is the power of that rare jewel—otherwise known as a good idea. As we've seen before, ideas are what propels this town and now more than ever even stars and directors are getting in on the idea-development game. Let's see who they are and how you can get your idea to them.

STARS AND DIRECTORS WITH PRODUCTION COMPANIES

Most of the "A list" stars—those who can get a "go" movie from the studios—have established their own independent production companies. These include the biggest, most bankable performers in the business, all of whom (unless they only see finished scripts) actively pursue ideas to develop into movies. Production companies give you the opportunity to submit material without relying only on the star's agent. Generally, the assumption is that the agent much prefers to deal in scripts; agents want their clients working as opposed to waiting it out while the project is being written. However, if you really do have a character idea or great subject matter particularly suited to a specific star or director, there is a possibility that by contacting that person's production company you can pitch your idea to him or her. If the star or director likes it, your idea is immediately salable to a studio.

In the appendix of this book, I've supplied you with a list of stars and directors who have their own companies and the addresses of those companies. (Do bear in mind that because the entertainment industry changes so rapidly, some of the studio-based production companies may have moved and will no longer be at the address provided.) If you're looking for a name and do not find the artist listed, you may be able to get further information by contacting any of the larger agencies and inquiring as to who represents that artist and whether or not there is a production company address available.

Whether you go this route alone or you have a producer— someone who functions as I do—taking your idea around, these players make the process easier because they are, for the most part, very creative people who enjoy collaborating and developing ideas. A star can champion an idea and thereby assuage the studio's fears about the riskiness of the venture. Some stars are especially interested in taking risks —in expanding their character range. *Rain Man,* as an example, wasn't thought to be a commercial property. Yet Dustin Hoffman, who wanted to tackle the difficult role of the autistic savant, helped to be a part of the strong package that got the movie made.

How much tailoring you should do for stars and directors can be answered by the following guidelines:

IDEAS FIRST

I wouldn't want to encourage you to spend most of your time developing your ideas for certain stars or directors. As you are coming up with story elements, you may want to depict a character as "a Tom Hanks type" or describe the style of the movie as having "a Mel Brooks tone." This is great for your process anyway, since you can always throw these tidbits into a pitch later on. In fact, the more vivid such details are in the telling, the better the pitch. Still, it would probably be counterproductive to sit at home and limit your imagination by coming up with an idea that only fits Tom Hanks or that only Mel Brooks could direct.

When I am given a very strong idea, for instance, I usually take it and pitch it first to the studios, knowing they'll want to choose the star. In the case of a good but marginal idea, I'll try to get a star attached.

And now, to get down to the brass tacks of packaging, here is an authoritative viewpoint.

AN AGENT'S PERSPECTIVE

I talk regularly with several agents at the Bauer-Benedek Agency, which has a long list of clients and credits. They sold *Dog Day Afternoon* and *Presumed Innocent*, among others. They launched the Cohen brothers as writers/producers and represent director Martin Bregman, who has a deal at Universal. They represent Brian De Palma and are involved in *Casualties of War*, *Body Double*, and *Bonfire of the Vanities*. They also represent Steve Kloves, the writer of *The Fabulous Baker*

Boys and *Racing with the Moon.* In his role as agent, one of the spokespersons for the agency said he considers himself to be both buyer and seller. He "buys" from writers and *sells* to studios.

In discussing *K-9*—which some refer to as "*48 Hours* with a cop and a dog"—he also mentioned to me that he had a story that was similar. How then, as an agent, would something like that get packaged? His response was that every project is different and first must be analyzed in detail by the agency to decide the best strategy. The script is next shown to a few key studio executives and a few of the key stars' agents to get an initial feel for the project.

One of the studio executives may decide that it's too much like something he's already got in development. Another may not understand the concept or fail to share the agency's enthusiasm for the script. Should these responses come back, the agent would opt not to show it to the studio, but to go out and get a Kathleen Turner or Jessica Lange or attach a director. You can probably guess that the next step is to go back to the studio and say, "Here's the script and look who's attached." (Yet there's sometimes a problem here—the studio may not like the players who have been attached!)

Because Sally Field is hot at Columbia, that won't mean Warner Brothers is dying to do a movie with her. "Star cache" rises and falls all the time and can vary from company to company. No one wants to saddle the project with a star who the studio feels doesn't draw an audience. So, in an ongoing dialogue with the studio executives, agents have to stay on top of the latest trends in the casting process—in addition to knowing what types of subject matter are hot. A recent advent in talent packaging is being heralded as "high-concept casting." Putting together director Susan Seidleman (of *Desperately Seeking Susan*) with Roseanne Barr and Meryl Streep for *The Life and Loves of a She-Devil* was allegedly done along these lines.

The agents I talked to have also worked with some properties that were infinitely packageable. The script for *I Love You to Death* was so strong that Larry Kasdan got it on a Tuesday and was committed to do the project by Thursday. Barry Levinson commissioned a writer on a script called "Sniper" based on a concept so vivid that the publicity log-lines could be envisioned the minute it was described. Sometimes a project like this can be put together and sold in twenty-four hours.

Echoing my belief about what sells in Hollywood, these agents assert that, from their standpoint, passion for a project is a prerequisite. After that, an agent must know the buyer's likes and dislikes in order to assess which client's work will make for the best match. Knowing what the producers and directors have done in the past, what was successful for them, and what stars were assets—all is necessary information for agents and for would-be producers.

As you saw, my success with getting *Commando* to Joel Silver derived from such an awareness. Everyone in Hollywood knows that the big names in action/adventure are Joel Silver and Larry Gordon, who did *48 Hours* and *Die Hard*. It wouldn't make much sense to go to Joel Silver with a Tom Stoppard script. On the other hand, to illustrate how some people go for a wide range of properties it should be noted that Larry Gordon also did *Field of Dreams*.

To get another point of view on packaging, we should probably turn next to:

THE WRITER'S VOICE

Hillary Carlip is a writer who successfully employed the principles of packaging to help get her first deal. While chatting with friends about dancing, Hillary observed that among teenage girls during the days of racial upheaval in the 1960s dancing was a form of establishing hierarchy, acting out rivalry, and overcoming differences. In fact, as a friend pointed out, back in her high school in New York, there were girl gangs that—instead of having rumbles like the guys— would have dance-offs. Although she began a screenplay and even went to New York to research the phenomenon, it wasn't until 1988 that she actually did anything with the idea. At that time, Hillary teamed up with Katie Ford, an established television writer who was on hiatus from her position as executive story editor on "Family Ties." The two wrote the script, which tells of two teenage girl cousins from different economic levels—one from uppercrust Scarsdale who comes to stay with the other in the rougher terrain of the Bronx. The story is set against the backdrop of the 1964 New York World's Fair and mixes in this fascinating form of expression through the dances of the day.

Since we'll soon talk about the relative importance of a title, it may be interesting to note how the title for this project was found. Wanting to emphasize the element of this being a story about young women, Hillary used a thesaurus to look for different slang terms or reference words about women. Hence the title, "Skirts."

The first stage of packaging "Skirts" was to bring the project to producer Paul Aaron. The next step was to attach Kenny Ortega as director. His career as choreographer on such films as *Dirty Dancing* was going strong, but this was his first shot at the director's spot. There was some debate as to whether the choice of a first-time director made for a better package, but since the writers also had a previous professional and social relationship with Ortega, they maintained that having him on the movie would protect their vision. Writers, director, and producer all were represented by the Creative Artists Agency (CAA). In this situation, the packaging was done before the script was even brought to the agency. There was further speculation as to whether attaching a star was essential, but all parties decided to do without that. Now the studio could cast with all new, unknown talent, which might appeal to the studio's budget considerations. Once all these elements were in place, it took about a week to get the movie sold. Five studios wanted the project and Columbia ultimately made the deal. At that point, the studio executives could attach the star of their choice and—in this instance—added the pop singer/actress Debbie Gibson as part of the Columbia package. Although the project is now in turnaround (the term used when a studio's option period to make the movie has lapsed), the writers stand to gain even more financially if and when "Skirts" is picked up by another studio and finally made. Carlip and Ford give credit to the producer and agent for making them the best possible deal.

This example shows that a writer's voice can be heard in the packaging process and that it behooves the screenwriter or idea person to be aware of the benefits as well as the detriments.

Sometimes an established writer will be viewed as part of someone else's package. There are cases when the deal has been all set up, the studio has all of the elements—a major star, a director, a producer—and they come looking for a writer. Upon occasion, they will interview a number of writers until they decide who they want for the project. And yet, in certain situations the studio can't find a writer who will take the job. How does this happen? Who would turn down so much money? It happens when the idea is lousy, for starters, and the smart writers are in positions to pick and choose projects that will better their careers. In such a packaging situation, the writer will have the foresight to see that no matter how much money is paid, this lousy idea is probably going to make a lousy movie.

Writers who are known as script doctors—who fix and rewrite a troubled, problematic script—can make as much as $50,000 to $100,000 a week. But there are projects that even these heavy hitters will turn down. One such writer turned down doing a "polish" on a major star script because he felt no matter how much the studio offered, it still wasn't worth putting his name on what he felt was going to be an inferior movie.

The freedom and power that come with being a packageable writer is, obviously, desirable. But first that reputation must be earned either with the quality of your screenwriting or with the marketability of your ideas.

And before we move on to the next stage of the game— the pitch—we should examine one minor question:

WHAT ARE YOU GOING TO CALL IT?

The importance of having a good title is not a serious concern. On one hand, if you have a sensational high-concept title that in a few words can tell your audience what the movie is about and also get them intrigued, then yes, that title is going to be an excellent selling tool for your idea. *Blind Date* comes up as a prime example once again. *K-9* strikes a similar chord.

On the other hand, a good title is no substitute for a weak premise or an uninteresting idea. You might get a response like, "That's a great title, but what's the story?" It would be very unlikely for you to sell a project based on the strength of the title.

With these considerations in mind, I would still recommend that you come up with some sort of working title. You needn't rack your brain for a brilliant title, but at least have something to throw out so that the listener can make a mental or written note about the project. When in doubt, use a generic title or your protagonist's name. Call it "The Airport" —if your story takes place in such an arena; or "Mildred"— if that's the name of the female lead.

Movies have been bought, shot, and released with mediocre, misleading, or silly titles and have still been successful.

Also, be aware that titles often are changed many times during preproduction. The film originally produced as "Little Havana," with Jimmy Smits and director Gillian Armstrong, was retitled "Distant Shores" and then finally given the title *Fires Within* for its release.

Suffice it to say if you can find a clever, catchy title for a good idea . . . that's icing on the cake. And with that food metaphor, let me add it's now time to proceed to the main course.

"Brevity is the soul of wit."

—William Shakespeare

"Time is money."

—One of life's great truths that
always applies in Hollywood

There is a pertinent comment attributed to Dan Melnick, the producer of such acclaimed films as *Network* and *All That Jazz*. From this respected filmmaker comes this observation: If you play the Hollywood pitch game, you inevitably will be made to feel like a rug merchant. This is not meant to demean the value of those worthy individuals who sell carpeting. But the fact remains, when you run around with your wares (your ideas), you are, unfortunately, in the same position as the rug merchant or vacuum cleaner salesperson. Once your project is sold or if you're lucky and it becomes a hit, everyone will call you a genius or perhaps even an artist. Until then, though, we all have to find ways to elevate ourselves and somehow not be seen as a pest. And don't be discouraged by any of the following unpleasant realities.

EVERYONE'S LOOKING TO SAY NO

Why is this so? Because of the age-old truth emblazoned at the beginning of this chapter and in the hearts and minds of everyone in Hollywood: *Time is money.* If an executive takes on your project, it's going to mean more time and more work; chances are that executive already has plenty of work and no time. Beyond this, as we previously stated, Hollywood has rather strict guidelines for what it doesn't want. It is also much riskier to say yes rather than no. So at the earliest opportunity, you will be told no, if you are taking up too much time and/or you bring up one of those no-no subjects.

Your first task, then, becomes to avoid this Hollywood predisposition. Don't come in with a typical drug story, a tired murder mystery, or a "disease of the week" plot. Whatever you do, do not be boring! The key phrases, which we'll repeat throughout this chapter and that you should engrave in your mind, are: *Be brief* and *Be enthusiastic.*

Just like Shakespeare says, *brevity* can do no wrong. We've talked all along about the one-liners and the beauty of simplicity in an idea. I hope by this stage you'll have honed a few of these essential basics. Continue to condense and concentrate the story elements; know how to highlight only the salient plot points; edit out all extraneous details. When you waver or wander, you can be saved by the second pitch ingredient—*sheer enthusiasm.*

When asked how I would describe my style in three adjectives, I once responded: "Enthusiastic, passionate, and even more passionate." My approach was described in the *Los Angeles Times* as telling bedtime stories to adults. Well, that's correct in that I attempt to hold my audience in suspended disbelief—as if they were playing make-believe along with me. As far as "bedtime" goes, though, if someone were to actually fall asleep during my pitch . . . then I would be doing something very wrong.

To keep your buyer from losing interest and to give yourself an added boost of enthusiasm, tell your idea *as if* it were already up on the screen. Your conviction and believability will entice your listener and supply something very powerful that figures into our next rule of the pitch game:

EVERYBODY IS LOOKING FOR THEIR NEXT HIT

Bear in mind that the person on the other side of the desk—no matter who he or she may be—isn't so different from you. Understand that even though everyone is looking to say no, this latest theory overrides the first one. If you walk into that office as if you've got the next best thing to *E.T.*, your buyer just might forget the word *no*.

I'm well aware that many screenwriters and idea people experience nervousness when entering the lion's den. Some of the best writers in the world have asked me to pitch for them, just because they dread being forced to tell their stories briefly and without the written word. Once, my producing partner and I were horrified when a screenwriter we'd brought in with us to pitch literally froze. Unable to speak or move or remember one word of his well-developed story, the writer was even more humiliated than we were. Luckily, we knew the important features of the plot and were able to take over for him.

Other idea people, while managing to maintain their powers of speech, can begin to drone on and on about the story. This can even happen to well-prepared individuals who might react badly to being "put on the stand." While these skittish feelings are certainly understandable, they can be overcome if you remember the following two points.

First of all, the sale is not dependent on an ability to pitch well. The sale depends on the quality of the idea. So if, indeed, you feel weak when it comes to pitching—take heart. A clear, intelligent, straightforward approach is far better than going in and wowing your audience with a dazzling performance. Besides, you'll always have the option of getting someone who is in my position to take your idea on and pitch it for you.

The other reason that it's important to overcome "pitch-fright" has to do with the fact that many executives are just as nervous as you. If you go into the office acting ill at ease, you're going to make someone who's already under enormous pressure feel even worse.

The best way to tackle nerves is to practice your pitch at home with a friend or in front of a mirror. Concentrate at all times on the key words: *brevity* and *enthusiasm*.

As you know by now, I often suggest the use of three-by-five cards. (This is the way I prefer to have ideas submitted to me.) They not only help you assess whether your idea meets the challenge of brevity, but they are also excellent pitching guides. A three-by-five card can be used as a cue card of sorts, so that you don't lose your momentum during the meeting and forget what originally excited you about the idea. Even if you never refer to the cards and leave them in your pocket or briefcase, they'll have definitely been helpful.

Make sure that you know each of the categories on this pitch checklist:

- The title
- The subject matter; genre and arena
- Premise in a one- to three-line summary
- Story/plot in a breezy overview

It's probably helpful at this stage to forget all the analogies about buying and selling and all the knowledge you have about what kind of power the studio executive holds. The best metaphor here is that of the game. You're going to be tossing ideas around in an enjoyable way and hoping that the listener agrees that one of the ideas could be a hit.

Next let's discuss your potential teammate.

THE HIERARCHY OF STUDIO EXECUTIVES

The titles that are listed next will vary from studio to studio, so you should always check first with your agent or the executive's assistant if you need an exact title. The ranking which follows tells you little other than the fact that the higher up the executive, the fewer channels you'll have to follow after your initial pitch. On the other hand, the slightly lower level executives are also the ones who are usually the most receptive. Many of these junior executives are as ambitious as you are and will really fight for your idea. The success of your project will often help them as much as you.

. . . .

LOWEST LEVEL

Creative Executive
Development Executive
Production Executive

LOW LEVEL

Director of Development
Director of Creative Affairs

MIDDLE LEVEL

Vice President of Feature Production
Vice President of Creative Affairs
Senior Vice President of Feature Production

UPPER LEVEL

Executive Vice President of Feature Development

. . . .

It's my feeling that you shouldn't alter your style no matter who you're pitching to. The few exceptions will bring only minor variations, such as:

The Total Pro

These are the executives who listen to pitches all day long, day in and day out. In these cases, I recommend that you take brevity and cut it in half. These pros at the pitch process don't need to hear any embellishing whatsoever. Give them the concept and go on to the next. If you're telling the plot, cut right to the chase. I personally happen to enjoy these situations, since we are in sync; these executives speak my language of "pitch shorthand." I know they understand and recognize a good concept.

The Cautious Conservative

Whether new to the position or already established as playing it very safe, an executive with this demeanor may need some special consideration. I would be careful with both the subject matter and the pace at which you present your ideas. It may be better in such instances to simply slow down and elaborate. Here I suggest you stick to one or two ideas.

The Specialist

This will be that situation when you are there just to discuss one idea. Be well versed in the story and characters that go along with your concept.

Keeping all these nuances in mind, we're going to be doing a mock-up of a standard pitch meeting. We'll call you "You" and the executive "The Executive." (How's that for clever?)

    You'll also see that I've given you five concepts to pitch. Two of them should be very familiar. The third is an idea that belongs to two writers from Rick Pamplin's class and has already been sold. The fourth is one of mine that has already been sold and produced as a TV movie. The fifth is an idea that hasn't sold. But for the sake of believability in playing out the following scenario, suppose these ideas all belong to you and that they haven't been seen anywhere before.

• • • • • • • • • • • • • •

YOUR FIRST PITCH MEETING

FADE IN ON:
You, seated in the outer office at the studio, waiting for your appointment with The Executive. You glance at your watch. Even though you were five minutes early, you are being kept waiting for an extra fifteen minutes to demonstrate how important the executive is and how unimportant you are. During this time (which can be longer) you practice your ideas in your mind.

CUT TO:
The executive's office. It is very nice. You comment on it, after shaking hands.

                    YOU
Great office!

                  THE EXECUTIVE
Thanks.

(picking up intercom)

Hold all calls.

(He'll say this if you're having a lucky day!)

You have a little improv or improvisation here, a couple of minutes of what is called foreplay or social bonding where you chitchat about how his tennis game is going. How long have he and his girlfriend been dating? How is the studio doing with such and such a movie, which you loved? Eventually, after two or three minutes of semi-humorous patter, one of you will bring up the topic of your ideas that you've brought to pitch. You remember that you are going to be animated and upbeat.

                    YOU
I've got some ideas that I'm really excited about. What I'd like to do is run the concepts by you very briefly and then we can go back and talk about the ones that interest you.

               THE EXECUTIVE
Sounds okay to me.

This is a good way to introduce your plan of action. Give each concept no more than thirty to sixty seconds. Usually, you won't get to pitch five ideas, but you'll note in this case that the executive starts to enjoy the meeting. Normally, you'll also want to pitch as many genres as possible, covering all the bases. In this particular pitch meeting, however, you've mostly got comedies, which may work to your disadvantage.

                    YOU
Great. This first one is a romantic comedy. See, this guy falls in love with the perfect woman, but she just happens to be a mermaid.

               THE EXECUTIVE
(chuckling)
What are you calling it?

                    YOU
Oh, I call that "Splash." The next one is also a comedy. The premise is basically a variation on *Some*

Like It Hot. A man can't get a job so he dresses up as a woman, then falls in love with someone who doesn't know he's really a man. Oh, I only have a working title for now—"Tootsie."

> THE EXECUTIVE
> Hmmm. What's next?

Let me mention here that when I sit opposite these executives, I play the game as if they are virtually daring me to come up with something different. I'll open with a line such as the one you are about to use.

> YOU
> This one's really different and very suspenseful. I doubt whether you've ever heard anything like this. The tag line might be: "A love story between a man who's afraid of everything and a woman who's afraid of nothing."

> THE EXECUTIVE
> Cute. Let's come back to that one. Have any more?

> YOU
> Two more. This fourth one is called "Dream Date." It asks the question: What is every father's worst nightmare? Your daughter's first date.

(The executive nods and makes a note on a scratch-pad.)

> YOU
> And this last one is a comedy/fantasy. Picture the poster: "They're young, they're in love, and they're on their honeymoon. Destination: Earth."

THE EXECUTIVE

It's a great line, but too expensive for us right now.
We've already got something like it anyway. Go
back to the third and fourth ideas. What's this one
about—the one between a man who's afraid of
everything and a woman who's afraid of nothing?

(at this point you begin to tell the story)

This was called "Stepping Out" and came from Silverman
and Schuyler, two writers in one of Rick Pamplin's classes. It
was pitched to three or four different studios and they all
wanted it. In this scenario we've described, the executive is
very interested and you summarize the story, which
shouldn't take more than two or three minutes. He tells you
that he'll get back to you later about "Stepping Out" and
then asks about the dad's nightmare and the daughter's first
date. As you describe it, emphasize the premise and tell the
simple story.

YOU

It's a funny setup. Picture a Chevy Chase type
going from one disaster to the next . . . while his
daughter has the perfect dream date. All that paranoia he had in the first place proves to be un-
founded. So he learns in the end to trust his
daughter.

It's good to point out that the character goes through some
kind of growth, though you don't want to overdo your character description so that it outweighs the plot. Nor can you
really go into a script dialogue in your pitch. In this scenario,
however, you have done extremely well.

THE EXECUTIVE

(shaking his head and laughing)
Yeah, my dad almost did the same thing to my sis-
ter—only he sent me to spy on her instead!

CUT TO:
You, the next day at home, getting a phone call to come back in on the "Dream Date" idea. It looks like you might just have a deal.

This, of course, was an all-around perfect situation in which an executive could recognize the universal aspects inherent in your idea and even had a personal reference point which made the premise more meaningful to him. Let's now take a look at some less than optimal circumstances taken from the annals of bad pitching and see if you can pinpoint the miscellaneous errors committed by the idea people.

• • • • • • • • • • • • • • •

THE ONE-IDEA PITCH

We open on an uncomfortable meeting under way between Ms. Young (the executive) and a writer who goes by the name of Reggie, who is quivering visibly.

MS. YOUNG
So, Reggie, your agent tells me you've got a hot project in the works. By the way, our readers were very impressed with your sample script. Unfortunately, we're not interested in westerns at the moment.

REGGIE
Right. Well, don't you worry. This new one is totally contemporary. Mainstream, high-concept, a star vehicle.

(starts flailing his arms erratically)

We're talking about an actress's dream role. Michelle Pfeiffer, Meg Ryan, Meryl Streep, Madonna. . . .

CLOSE UP ON:
Ms. Young's face. Her eyebrows rise with interest.

> MS. YOUNG
> Excellent. We're always looking for a good woman's story, especially for actresses whose names begin with M. . . .

> REGGIE
> Funny you should mention that, since my film is called "M." It's a remake of *Dial M for Murder* with a woman in the Ray Milland role.

CLOSE UP ON:
Ms. Young's face. Obviously, she isn't familiar with this 1950s Hitchcock thriller.

> MS. YOUNG
> Ray Milland—wasn't he terrific as Shoeless Joe in *Field of Dreams?*

> REGGIE
> I think you mean Ray Liotta—

> MS. YOUNG
> (interrupting)
> Refresh my memory—what's the premise?

> REGGIE
> In my version, a woman has an assassin kill her husband but then falls in love with the cop who comes to investigate the murder.

> MS. YOUNG
> Didn't I see something like that on "Kojak"?

REGGIE

No, this is much more suspenseful. You see, the cop, as it turns out, is actually a con guy, an escaped felon, disguised as a cop. So, in the end, when the wife and the felon/cop get together, it's because they are such lousy individuals they deserve each other. It's very climactic, with a chase scene that starts at a mall, moves to Sea World, connects up with a group of dolphins who have made contact with a colony on Mars, and then actually ends up on Mars. The message is about the environment. You see, the intrinsic evil of this couple pollutes our world and then corrupts the dolphins and then instills the germ of evil on Mars. . . . What do you think?

CLOSE UP ON:
Ms. Young's face. She has fallen asleep.

MS. YOUNG
(suppressing a yawn)

Do you have anything else?

FADE OUT AS:
Reggie sadly shakes his head, collects his things, and leaves.

   While this scenario may seem far-fetched, much more convoluted ideas than our example have been pitched. Reggie would have been in a better position if he at least had had another pitch ready as a backup, even though you'll rarely get a chance to pitch more than one or two. If you are going in with one great concept that is really well detailed, spend ten to fifteen minutes on it in an authoritative, animated, and articulate way. Even when I pitch more than five ideas, I never spend more than fifteen to twenty minutes in the office. Do not take more than half an hour on any idea.

Television- and screenwriter Will Rogers (no relation to the legendary cowboy) had an experience that drove home the belief that one idea isn't enough, in addition to another issue. See if you can pinpoint it in the next sketch.

•••••••••••••••

THE ONE-SECOND PITCH

The theme music from *Rocky* plays and credits roll as cutting shots show a Writer at work over the period of several weeks. Various notebooks, scratchpads, action graphs on easels, shots of him researching subject matter by a seedy wharf, the writer practicing his pitch in front of a mirror. Credits end as music changes to *Jaws* shark refrain. The Development Person enters his own office as the writer stands to shake hands.

>   DEVELOPMENT PERSON
> Whatcha got?

>   WRITER
>   (very proud)
>
> "Die Hard II" on a boat.

>   DEVELOPMENT PERSON
> Nah, just read it. What else do ya got?

CUT TO:
Horrified expression on the writer's face. Matching shots of horrified faces from outtakes of various horror films, such as *Psycho* and *Nightmare on Elm Street*. Ending credits roll as the writer strings up his own noose.

If you guessed that this fictitious writer's problem was his one-liner, then you guessed right. In and of itself, there's nothing disastrously wrong with using such a line. But in this case, it didn't pique the imagination of the executive and the writer, as with Reggie, didn't have any other cards to play.

For Rogers, the real-life writer, a very similar real-life encounter made him aware of the limitations of the one-liner. To reiterate my earlier stance on employing these lines, let's recall that they are, at best, tools. Very rarely will they absolutely determine an instant sale. So rather than spending all your time researching and developing a strong story only to blow it off with a weak one-liner (that someone else has probably just pitched), divide your energies by coming in with two or three different story setups.

Also, as agent Vik Malo points out, a typical pitfall for the novice is in trying to pitch what Malo calls "unexplained character sympathy." Writers and idea people can create unlikable protagonists and expect the listener to believe an audience will care about what happens to the character. "Why do we like this guy?" Malo often asks clients. "We just do" is usually the response, one that this agent and others will criticize as unacceptable.

Let's assume for the next vignette that the pitch person, Marie, has had a positive first pitch meeting and has been called in for a second meeting with Mr. Creative (the Development Executive) to focus in on story elements. This particular idea was actually used in the film originally called "Filofax," which became *Taking Care of Business*, and probably was conceived and presented in the way that Marie has:

• •

"What is every corporate yuppie's worst nightmare? He loses his daily organizer."

• •

What happens, though, during Marie's follow-up story meeting is that she hasn't worked out the story elements beyond the premise. Here she will be given an opportunity to take advantage of Mr. Creative's input, but she just may or may not be prepared for the suggestions he'll make.

·················

THE FOLLOW-UP SECOND MEETING

We open with a shot of the busy executive's messy desk. Papers are strewn over it, along with several empty Styrofoam coffee cups and two ashtrays overflowing with cigarette butts. Marie, a tidy, prim type, looks askance at the disorder, but the executive doesn't seem to mind because he's . . .

> MR. CREATIVE
> (getting right down to business)
>
> Have you given some thought to the identity of the character who accidentally finds the organizer?

> MARIE
> Absolutely. What if the corporate person is a snooty woman boss in a stock brokerage and the person who gets hold of her organizer is a young, ambitious girl working in the lower ranks of the company? Using the organizer, the girl impersonates the boss when she goes away on vacation.

> MR. CREATIVE
> That's great, except for one thing. That's just about the exact same story line as *Working Girl*.

Marie swallows in embarrassment for not having seen that film.

MR. CREATIVE

(continuing)

What if the guy who loses the organizer is the son of the owners of a huge Wall Street firm where he also works? And he loses the book to a black guy who's grown up on the streets, who then takes over the firm while the rich guy is framed for a crime the black guy supposedly committed?

MARIE

Isn't that too much like *Trading Places?*

(smugly)

I saw that one.

MR. CREATIVE

How about this: The main guy is a computer whiz who has just come up with a program that his company is going to sell to the aerospace industry and the code is written in the daily organizer. He loses it and it's found by his son's best friend, a twelve-year-old kid, who also knows a lot about computers and with the code is able to infiltrate NASA and almost starts World War III.

MARIE

No. I conceived of this idea as a spoof on yuppies, not on young adolescents and certainly not to be used as a hack version of *War Games.*

MR. CREATIVE

(thankfully not listening)

I've got it. We'll do a time-travel thing. A guy from the future has amnesia and comes back in time and finds the organizer and poses as its owner and because he's from the future he has all this new technology at his disposal and makes a fortune for the real guy's company. I think my boss would really go for that. She's been looking for a time-travel thing. It's perfect.

CLOSE UP ON:
Marie's empty chair.

I'm often asked how to approach a situation such as Marie's in which an executive is interested in a concept but the story hasn't been worked out. When, as we just saw, the studio exec wants to take part in the creative process, the input should be welcomed. Collaborative rapport is one of the best things that can happen in the idea-selling process because it indicates that the executive has already made a personal investment in your idea.

The next best thing to you two hammering out the story together is when one of you suggests hiring a writer for the idea. This is fine with the studio, the rationale being that writers get paid for story skills, so why not? Bring in that writer and team him or her up with this wonderful idea and the deal is made.

Alternatively, you may be told that the company doesn't want your idea unless you come back with the complete story plotted out. This is the studio's prerogative. Unfortunately for them, you then have the choice of taking your idea around the corner and pitching it to a less demanding executive. If the concept is as good as you think it is, the second studio will buy it and the first will have lost out.

I should advise you that studios may request a written story synopsis when they are ready to seal the deal. This can be a one-page outline of the idea and is usually satisfactory. If you are required to write out the complete story, I suggest that you write three to ten pages covering your plot. Your style needn't be anything fancier than a sixth grade book report. The emphasis here is to ensure that everyone at all levels will "get" the story.

While Marie in the previous sketch certainly doesn't set an example of optimum collaboration, you may encounter your own resistance to creative assistance. From similar experiences, some idea people have concluded that certain ideas should not be pitched if you are going to resist any outside tampering.

Screenwriter Robert Harders, for example, who has sold projects both from scripts and from pitching ideas, feels that an idea about which you feel very personal or which has strong story elements that you don't want to see changed shouldn't be brought into a pitch meeting in the first place. In such an event, he recommends, the idea person should either write the spec screenplay or team up with a writer sympathetic to the original idea.

Harders's other suggestion about the overall pitch process, learned from earlier disillusioning scenarios, is not to go in with a preconceived idea of what the particular executive wants. Being true to your own tastes and sensibilities is far more advantageous than trying to bluff your way through something that you think someone else is going to find more commercial.

Screenwriter and film director Teresa Sparks has, like Harders, sold projects both by submitting spec scripts and pitching ideas. Her idea for "Berlin," a Romeo and Juliet story set in the rock music scene of Berlin, was bought by an executive at Aaron Spelling Productions halfway through Ms. Sparks's first pitch. One ingredient alone, she claims, made it possible for the executive to interrupt the story and say, "I want to buy this," and that, Sparks says, was a good story.

When next she successfully pitched and sold the idea for "Hong Kong Baby" to Chestnut Hill Productions, where it is currently being developed, she attributed other pitching strengths as helpful. In addition to a clear and unique story, Sparks stresses the importance of approaching the pitch in a very straightforward manner. "I am not an actress," says this writer, "so I don't try to be one. I go in and simply tell the story." From her perspective, it is also valuable to have a personal stake in the subject matter. This doesn't mean pitching autobiographical ideas, but rather those that are relatable to the screenwriter or idea person.

Beyond the advice of pitching veterans from whom we've heard, let's explore some further "what if" questions that may arise.

Q: *What if the story is very complicated?*

A: If you think you need to lay out some additional information, you can always start by saying something like, "Let me give you some background and then we'll go right to the premise." Executives appreciate it when you are aware of their limited time schedule.

When you focus on a particular scene and you've become a set decorator and you're talking about the camera angle and the expression on the character's face and the theme of determinism versus free will and the movie's message concerning political optimism . . . the executive will quickly lose all interest. When I sit on the buying side of the desk, I usually ask the person pitching to give me the premise first or a brief overview. Then, if I want to hear more, I'll start to ask questions. Unfortunately, a few people have come in and suddenly become hard of hearing, even as I continue to ask, "What's this about?" or "But what's the premise?" There have been one or two occasions when I've been forced eventually to stand up and say that the meeting has come to an end.

To avoid being shown the door, always be on the alert. Make sure your audience is with you every step of the way. Stop the minute you see someone's eyes glaze over, and then go on to something else.

Q: *What if the executive is having a bad day?*

A: It happens. If there are many distractions for the executive—the phone, the pressure, odd and sundry interruptions, a bad mood—try, without calling attention to these facts, to reschedule the meeting. Stop with one idea and say that you have some others which you'd like to pitch next week.

Q: *What if you are having a bad day?*

A: Repeat the strategy I've just given and get out of there. A downtrodden demeanor can make you a desperate, drowning dud. Desperation is the kiss of death. Need I say more?

Q: *What if you can't read the executive's reaction?*

A: Ask, in an upbeat way, how the idea sounds. If you get an ambiguous or negative response, you may want to inquire as to what seems to be wrong about the idea, which can then lead you to an insightful improvement. But don't get defensive or push your point. Don't take criticism personally. Allow the executive to have his or her opinion and then say, "I can understand how you feel, and since you mentioned it . . . I have another project that might interest you." A situation such as this proves how essential it is to have a backup of several ideas.

Q: *What if the executive raves about all your ideas and then is never heard from again?*

A: Yes, this happens frequently. As you gain more experience, you will learn to distinguish between genuine interest and show business hype. You may wish to remember film critic Pauline Kael's observation that Hollywood is a place where a person can die from encouragement. The studios can stroke you from here to eternity, but until they start talking about a deal, don't get your hopes up. (This goes for actors and directors as well as writers and idea people.)

We should recall that good news does come fast. If there is genuine studio interest, you or your agent will hear very quickly. On the other hand, don't give up on your idea if you don't hear from one or two executives. The tastes of another executive may be very different or you may even find that you'll be back to the first executive with the same idea at a later date and you'll get a deal on what was once rejected. It will all depend on what's happening in the market and on your undying passion for your concept.

Q: *Will you ever pitch more than five ideas?*

A: If you are either pitching to an agent or to a producer with whom you're hoping to partner before going to the studios, you'll want to have a dozen or more ideas ready. One good idea alone won't get you an agent or a trusting producer who wants to build a future with you.

An agent is concerned about two areas. First, whether you're going to be able to continually generate ideas, which of course means continually generating the agent's ten percent commission. Second, when your agent sets up a pitch meeting, it's implicit that you are going in as a representative of your agent's tastes—even as a representative of the rest of the agency's clientele. Your agent won't want to risk his or her reputation by using important studio connections on someone who might go in and undermine the agent's status.

The independent producer is less focused on how you pitch than on the ideas themselves. Usually, the producer will go in and pitch first, then bring you in to a follow-up meeting—either alone with the executive or the two of you together.

Having dealt with some of the different situations in which you might find yourself pitching, let's move on to some unusual options others have successfully employed, as we turn to:

ALTERNATIVES IN PITCHING

While we explore the many devices that have helped writers and idea people obtain their deals, bear in mind that there is no substitute for substance. In other words, if you do not have an exciting idea or a unique story, a $100,000 theatrical presentation of the project is not going to guarantee your deal. However, by going the extra mile or possibly spending an extra nickel (okay, a little bit more than that), you can grab the attention of money-minded executives. This, in turn, will get you past the first hurdle where everyone is looking to say no. Almost everyone enjoys a diversion from their routine, and so your unusual way of breaking up the humdrum day probably will be welcomed.

Here we should again remember that selling to Hollywood is a numbers game. Realize that studio executives are listening to pitches day in and day out; their desks are piling up with more and more scripts, proposals, and treatments. So yes, if you can find a clever, entertaining, or catchy way to separate your project from the rest, then you should be able to rise above your competition.

The first category of alternatives is both the broadest and most prevalent in the industry. Since film is a visual art, the following techniques have proven extremely helpful to many veterans of the process:

The Video Pitch

Some years ago, David Permut and I had a not-so-successful pitch meeting with Sean Daniel, then president of production at Universal Pictures. "Gee," we joked as we were leaving without a sale, "you really should consider this idea. After all, we drove all the way to the Valley from Culver City to pitch it."

Waving us off, Sean suggested as a humorous retort that

we'd do better the next time if we sent him a videocassette. Everyone had a good laugh. But when David and I got back to the parking lot, we turned to one another with gleams in our eyes. Why not take the executive up on his challenge?

Our first step was to find one of our better ideas, which turned out to be the one created by Karen Hopkins called "The Favor." Then we hired a technical consultant, selected a location, and rented all the necessary lighting and camera equipment. To help with the event, our colleagues director Rick Pamplin and screenwriter John Bunzel came on board. Even Rick Pamplin's secretary, Betty Burns, was given a small cameo role. The cost of producing the video was somewhere in the vicinity of a thousand dollars.

In a generic Beverly Hills office, David Permut, John Bunzel, and I were seated on a sofa as I began the presentation by providing the premise: A shady fellow resurfaces in the life of an upstanding businessman and demands that a favor be repaid.

John then took over by telling ten minutes worth of the story, highlighting the more provocative twists and turns in the plot. From there, the focus went to David, who asked the intended audience to imagine such actors as Kevin Costner or Tom Hanks in the main role of the businessman and Danny DeVito or Jon Lovitz as the antagonist. At the tail end of the tape, Betty Burns announced the appropriate phone number to call just before we cut back to David. With utmost sincerity, he added, "And because of our special relationship, we're giving *you* the first look at our project."

Along with Sean Daniel at Universal, six other studio executives (because of our special relationship with each one) received a copy of the cassette. Several offers came back, but it was Paramount that bought the project. John Bunzel was hired to write the first draft, Karen sold her story, while David and I were attached as producers.

Since that sale, I personally haven't resorted again to the video pitch approach for the mere reason that it hasn't been necessary. Others have tried video pitching and gained equally satisfying results.

Posters and Pictures

Another common practice is to design and print posters of the unsold, unwritten, unproduced, unreleased movie *as if* it were coming soon to a theater near the executive.

I was easily interested, for example, in a project brought to me called "The Cad." In lieu of a pitch, the person who brought in the idea simply handed me a poster. On it was a black-and-white photo of a man and woman in shadows. Atop the photo were these words: "In 1940, when adultery was the only grounds for divorce, Hamilton Barth found himself practicing a peculiar profession. Seducing millionaires' wives at their husbands' requests. For a hundred thousand dollars a shot."

Below the picture were the title and tag lines: "THE CAD— A frightfully funny series of financial affairs."

I was impressed. I found that this was a project that I wanted to try to sell. In the event that you don't have the wherewithal to actually make a poster, you can try a "poor man's version" of the same technique. By verbally describing the poster, using lines such as those that appeared on the poster of "The Cad," you can basically achieve the same effect.

Variations on this theme have been reported by writers who "storyboard" their idea in cartoon form, set their blown-up four- or five-square comic strip on an easel, and point to the characters being described as the story is explained. Others have used their arts and crafts skills to create elaborate folders containing magazine pictures and marketing figures.

I'd venture to say that few executives are going to buy one project over another solely on the basis of a slick presentation. What will make the difference is your having taken the time to think about how your movie might be promoted. If you have zeroed in on a way to sell the idea to the public, it may bring the executive to the conclusion that there is a potentially profitable property within arm's reach.

If you haven't figured out a way your movie might be publicized, it often means that you yourself don't really know what the story is about. Go back again to the drawing board at home and ask what is the simplest way to convey the idea in a picture or in a few juicy ad lines. This should be well worth the effort, since poster pitching, whether with a bona fide poster or a verbal portrayal of it, is a strong sales tool.

Audio Pitching

Like its more expensive video version, an audiocassette tape will stand out from competing submissions of ideas. For a busy studio executive, who can stick it in a car tape player or a Walkman around the house, this offers a nice way to deal with hectic schedules. I have received submissions in this fashion which have employed music and sound effects behind the premise and story recap.

Although I have never pitched an idea via an audio tape, as I prefer the live encounter, I have used a minute or so of taped music right in an executive's office before launching into the pitch. You should note, however, as always, that a fantastic musical demonstration won't get a movie deal if the idea itself is weak.

Theater in the Round

Miscellaneous producers and screenwriters have been known to hire actors (or enlist the help of them) to be on hand for either a read-through of a partially written script or a skit that enacts the salient plot points of the story. Remember, anything that assists a viewer in imagining the reality of that idea up on the screen shouldn't be dismissed. In fact, many top executives like to see read-throughs of scripts during the course of a project's development.

Incidentally, there's nothing wrong with staging such a mock-up of the storytelling process if you are trying to iron out problems in the structure. Independent television producers with series ideas often bring in actors who can improvise action or who can help to flesh out characters.

The Spectacle

One of the most outlandish and elaborate alternatives to a standard pitch happened a few years back in the context of an idea being presented to a network executive. This particular idea was a comedy series set against the backdrop of the personal ad department of a newspaper. Before going in to do a live version of the pilot, the producers involved were able to find out the personal statistics of a couple of different network executives. Then they actually ran ads in a local paper that provided a P.O. box for readers who wanted to meet or date that single guy or gal.

Once the producers, writers, and actors finished their enactment of the idea, one of them revealed a blow-up of the ad that had run. Right away the executive could clearly see his own data. Here was the coup de grace: The producer held out a sealed manila envelope containing the letters that had arrived in response to the ad and promised to turn the envelope over *only* if the series was bought. What made this endeavor so remarkable was that the producers did it for two different executives—a single male and a single female. Which one would you guess actually bought the deal? If you guessed that it was the male who was ultimately moved to find out what kind of prospects existed in his romantic life, then you have been doing your sociological homework.

Without question, these kinds of strategies will at the very least come as a refreshing break in anyone's routine. Nevertheless, the flip side of such efforts is that they do not guarantee a network or studio purchase. Even independent producers who are able to raise $3 million or more in financing to make their movies will sometimes be unable to obtain an advance distribution deal. Then, when they invite all the distributors to a screening of the movie, they are, in essence, pitching the idea in its finished form.

The Star

Much more prevalent than the previous example is an approach I've used several times when a star has been attached to the project. Since we've covered the packaging steps taken to attach the star (or director), we'll assume that some of you will get this pitching opportunity at some time or another.

First of all, walking into almost any pitch meeting with a respected actor or director will alter the tone and content of the pitch. The mere entrance of the star into that office sets the mental gears of the studio executive into motion. Second, many packageable artists already have first-look deals at given studios, which means that the executives there are waiting for the right project for that artist.

As far as pitching to the stars themselves, I recommend shifting the standard pitch away from the plot point of view and orienting it to the main character's point of view. The actor who is listening to the story doesn't think along the same lines as the studio executive; the actor is concerned about what can be gained from playing the role you are pitching. Once you've established interesting character features, you'll also want to stress a strong story line since a star does care about the movie ultimately becoming a success, should he or she decide to become attached.

When William Blaylock and I took Jeff Silverman's true-life story of "The First Boy to Go to Vassar" to Michael J. Fox, he immediately liked the main character and the story. Equally important, Michael saw that we weren't trying to do a youth exploitation film about a young man going to an all-girl school to have a series of conquests. Sharing in our vision of wanting to do an intelligent adult comedy more along the lines of *Shampoo* or *Tootsie*, Michael saw the appeal of the project and was willing to attach his very prestigious name to it, as well as participate in the pitching process farther down the road.

I will admit, in passing, that in a few cases the presence of the star can get a deal from a pitch even with a mediocre idea. With Michael J. Fox on board, I got the impression that the studios would have made an offer even if he had been attached to the yellow pages. Fortunately, in that case, the idea was also a good one.

The lesson to be learned from this pitching alternative is that if you've attached a clout-wielding star, director, or writer and have a chance to take him or her with you to pitch, do it!

Ordinary People/Extraordinary Stories

In some cases, when you are pitching an idea based on a real-life person whose story rights you've bought, it is constructive to bring that individual to the pitch meeting. My project "Kick" was sold in this way, when ex-Rockette Marie Bowen joined me and presented her own story of her comedic adventures at Radio City Music Hall. Because Marie's experiences involved her overcoming the odds in a challenging situation, I was able to pitch the project as "Norma Rae with Long Legs." But what really heightened the desirability of the idea was Marie herself, in person, telling her wonderful and dramatic experiences from the days that she first struggled to become a Rockette to the time that she took on the entire oppressive system of her working world. My success in selling Marie's true-life story to Paramount was the combined result of a well-told and strong story and Marie's warm, accessible presence.

Let's not forget there are instances where a real-life person isn't as helpful during pitch meetings. Use your judgment as to whether you think someone whose story you've optioned is going to be comfortable pitching with you. Sometimes it's better to bring in the article that originally caught your attention or other press-related materials about the person.

Partner Pitching

It's always an interesting diversion when two or more people handle the standard pitch. Likewise, this is a fine way to combat the pressure of having to go into the shark pool all alone. You can trade off telling different parts of the story or play one character as your partner plays the other.

Craig Heller and Guy Shulman, a writing team that pitched to me recently, have a choreographed plan of action for each idea. They'll pass their movies' plotpoints back and forth effortlessly, often picking up where the other left off in midsentence. This makes the listening experience much more varied and entertaining.

When pitching comedy ideas in particular, partners do well when at least one has a way with jokes. For that matter, a sense of humor when pitching always helps and never hurts.

The Apple Polish

Only in a rare case or two can tactics such as sending flowers, cute and clever cookie baskets, or singing telegrams (all of which have been done in conjunction with selling ideas to Hollywood) produce anything other than an appreciative "thank you, but no thank you" note. Such obvious attempts to have an idea considered or a script read usually smack of desperation, a dreaded label you do not want associated with you or any potentially interesting projects you might have.

There are other, less blatant social niceties that I wouldn't discourage. A follow-up note to an executive thanking him or her for the input, even when a deal wasn't struck, isn't a bad practice. Nor is making the extra effort to become familiar with various executives' secretaries and assistants. (As it frequently occurs, secretaries and assistants are the next in line for executive positions.)

However you decide to approach pitching, whatever you do don't be a pest. While this should go without saying, many a producer or studio executive has been hounded ad nauseum by people who refuse to take no for an answer. I was plagued by one individual who, after pitching me an idea that I rejected, kept calling and writing daily for weeks on end, trying to inform me that I'd made a big mistake in not wanting to take on the idea. In the language of Hollywood, as in most languages, *no* means no. *No* can also mean, "No, I'm not interested, but maybe my neighbor is."

Success, as they say, is the best revenge. If someone has, in your estimation, rejected your idea unfairly, prove your worth by going to all the other buyers, or go-betweens, and matching your idea up with the tastes of the right person. Then, by the sheer virtue of your deal, you can say to everyone who turned you down along the way, "I told you so."

I must finally caution you: Some of the attention-getting tactics of alternative pitching can backfire so that the project comes under suspicion as being all hype. Slick song and dance routines can't hide the void created by the lack of substance.

THE BOTTOM LINE OF THE PITCH

Less is more. Your most important mission is to present an idea that is so exciting, so tantalizing, so imaginative that the listener wants to hear more to discover how this provocative premise will unfold. When you start your pitch, you are making a promise: This is going to be a larger-than-life experience. A strong concept which makes a studio executive envision the story and the characters coming alive will in turn motivate the exec to immediately grab your idea for fear that another studio will get it first.

When you are known as an imaginative, commercial idea person or writer, you'll be a sought-after commodity. And at that point, you'll want to know all the specifics of what I'm about to reveal.

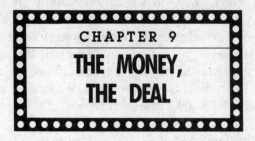

CHAPTER 9

THE MONEY, THE DEAL

"I don't care if you bring little puppies in here and pull out their nails one by one with pliers, I'm not changing one word of my script."

—From a conversation between a writer and
an exec at Disney in the late seventies;
otherwise called "How to Blow a Deal"

Horror stories such as this one abound in the industry. More than a handful of writers and idea people have sorely missed out on great opportunities because of inflated beliefs as to what their screenwriting abilities or their ideas are worth.

While you certainly don't want to underestimate the value of your idea or your screenwriting ability, you must have a realistic understanding of the financial side of the business.

Before we discuss what to expect in terms of money, credits, and deal structures—all for different types of projects—I want to present you with a scenario that illustrates the most commonly held prohibitive sentiment:

FEAR OF BEING FINANCIALLY SHORTCHANGED

This incident began a while back when I saw a story on the network news about a woman who billed herself as a housewife for hire. Having tracked her down and proposed that I try to sell her story, I received verbal permission from her to go ahead. Next I went to a production company and we all teamed up to try to sell the idea to the networks as a movie of the week. The offer for this woman's story was substantial: $50,000. However, as we explained to her, this wasn't the money that we could pay her up front. Once we'd sold the project to the networks and the movie was made, she would receive her full $50,000. She said, "No way!" She wanted the whole amount up front or no go.

Not being familiar with the standard way in which deals are made, she was paranoid about being ripped off. We explained that we weren't the networks, we were only the producers endeavoring to sell her story for her. As a compromise, we offered her $5,000 up front, but she still held fast to her demand for the $50,000. She blew her own deal. Ethically and legally, we couldn't proceed from there because we didn't own the rights to her story. And no one else in Hollywood went after her story. Before long, other people got wind of her housewife-for-hire true story, but also heard about other women who had launched the same sort of business. Then, once the studios knew that she wasn't the only one doing this routine, their legal advisors informed them it was unnecessary to buy the rights from this particular woman. Off the studios went, fictionalizing the stories without paying anyone. So you see, everyone lost out because of her shortsightedness. Because she was so sure that Hollywood was going to cheat her, she ended up cheating herself.

There are many writers who ended their careers before they'd begun because they were so fearful of being underpaid. They held out for the $200,000 which they never got, when they could have easily taken the $50,000 and begun a lifelong profession. Fear can stand in the way of a writer making that all-important first deal. Without the first deal, there obviously will not be any others.

To combat the fear of being cheated, let's discuss the dif-

ferent kinds of deals, as well as ballpark figures for compen-
satory monies and credits. (You should also refer to the
figures in the back of the book and read how to obtain further
information from the Writers Guild.)

THE DEVELOPMENT DEAL

While they may sound very complex, development deals are
actually quite simple and the studios do them every day.
Let's say you've pitched your idea or an intermediary producer such as myself has pitched the idea. The studio contacts you, your agent, or the producer to say they're
interested. Remember, if it's your idea, you control the underlying rights to the story. At this stage, negotiations begin
between a representative from business affairs at the studio
and your representative—your agent or lawyer.

You'll have some initial choices, all of which you must
negotiate with the studio:

- Do you want only to sell the story?
- Do you want to be hired to write the story?
- Do you want to attach yourself as part of the production
  entity?

You should, of course, use past deals as leverage to raise
your fee when negotiating your current deal. Similarly, you
will use past credits to begin moving up the credit ladder
(from associate producer to co-producer to producer). Your
lawyer, too, is going to try to make the best financial deal on
your behalf. Once the deal is closed you either receive money
for having sold the idea or you receive money to begin writing the screenplay.

When you sell your idea, you receive up-front option
money. You may receive a story bonus when the writer is
signed, and a larger bonus when the movie goes into pro-

duction. You will also receive a salary during production if you are attached as a producer.

The option period will usually be for six to eighteen months. During this time, the studio owns the rights to develop your idea either with you as the writer or with the writer they choose to hire. Now the script is "in development" and the studio owns it with you. If, over that time, no script is written that meets with studio approval, the project reverts back to you. You are then legally allowed to sell it again if you have the proper turnaround clause in your contract.

I have sold many of my projects this way more than once. When a studio develops an idea, it doesn't mean that they can own it forever. They own it only during the time they have it under option. When the option period is over, the project can revert to you in what is known as turnaround. When a script goes into turnaround, you usually have at least one year to try to sell it to another buyer, provided you pay the original studio the amount of money it has spent developing the script.

Frequently, when a good script goes into turnaround, you can easily set it up at another studio and they will take care of the turnaround costs.

The standard period allowed contractually for turnaround is one year to eighteen months. A two- to three-year (or longer) turnaround period is preferable and usually is given to more established writers or producers. This means that you—as the creator, writer, or producer—have a longer amount of time for another studio to pick up the project or for the original studio to decide to go ahead and make the movie. Once turnaround is over, if you have been unable to sell it to another buyer, the rights to the project revert to the original studio. If, say, at a later date someone becomes interested in buying the property, a purchase can be negotiated for more or less the original developmental costs. Again, every contract is different. Sometimes, on the same contract, the turnaround period specified to sell the project for a television series will be different from the turnaround for the feature film rights. These complexities point out the need for a lawyer or agent at this stage of the game.

When a hot property is in development, sometimes when there is a top star or major director attached, the studio may send "pay or play" notifications. This is good news, meaning that the studio is gearing up to go into production. If anything stands in the way of making the "play" (the playing out of the movie), the studio is promising to pay everyone attached their salaries.

Upon the first day of principal photography, a story creator can receive a story bonus payment. Later, there may be an arbitration to determine what credit you should receive on the screen. If you receive sole screenwriter credit, you will receive X amount of dollars; as a shared screenwriter, you'll get a bonus of a lesser amount. Ideas will usually yield the following credits:

- For a feature film   "Story by . . ."
- For a television movie   "Story by . . ." or
                              "Based on a story by . . ."
- For a television series idea
  and original treatment   "Created by . . ."

You probably realize that every deal is going to be different from the next. Each will have subtle and complicated clauses and provisions. And although we can't explore such a myriad of legal details, I hope this discussion gives you a practical sense of how a basic deal works.

DOLLARS AND CENTS: IDEAS AND SCRIPTS

As you've no doubt assumed, having the completed script is the best way to make the most up-front money. The range of monies regularly paid to option a script is between $10,000 and $100,000. If your script is produced, you will then receive an amount anywhere between $100,000 and $500,000.

You'll remember one of our first examples was Karen Hopkins, who brought me the idea for "Peep Show." This enabled her to get an agent and later she received over $250,000 from Paramount for an original screenplay.

With a strong idea, you can make $5,000 to $10,000 for the option of the idea. This means that every time the option is renewed, you will be paid that option money to keep the idea at the studio as it is being written. Your story bonus money due on the first day of principal photography will fall into the $10,000 to $50,000 range. If you have been attached as part of the production entity—either as co-producer or as associate producer—you stand to receive another $10,000 to $50,000 in salary money.

This financial incentive should suggest to you why I strongly favor having more than one idea. If you can get various projects optioned around town, you'll both increase your income and increase your chances that one or more ideas will get made.

The option arrangement from the studio is always made with the person who owns the story. Even when a producer has brought your story to the studio, you can make the deal and you negotiate the option.

There is another important financial consideration:

Points

In certain circumstances, you may have managed to be included in a share of the net profits. Perhaps you'll have a net point or two. A net point is literally one one-hundredth of the total net profits. Then, if the movie makes $50 million to $100 million, you'll be looking at another payoff of $200,000 to $300,000. But rarely, unless this movie is a huge blockbuster, will that $50 million to $100 million show up in net profits. Why? Because once the movie has earned what it cost to make, market, and distribute (meaning it has broken into profit), the first people to earn percentages are those who've been given gross points. After all the gross players have been paid their percentage, the studio can often show that there isn't profit yet for the net players. Profit participation and studio accounting are controversial subjects in Hollywood, where "creative accounting" is sometimes hard to understand.

Profit participation breaks down in two ways: gross points and net points. As you ascend the ladder of success and become more established, you can demand the more preferable of the two—gross points. If you've been given gross points, you can receive your percentage (your points) the minute the film brings profit to the studio. In contrast, a net player will not realize profits until much later, when the film is said to go into official profit. This is why most people (especially beginners) receive net points. These net point participants rarely see any money from their points unless they have net points in a blockbuster movie.

Variations in Television

The size of fees one can receive from TV movies is a scaled-down version of what we've discussed in the feature world. From $500 to $5,000 is the going rate to option your idea. A bonus of approximately $5,000 can be expected when a writer is hired. When the project goes into production, you can receive a story bonus of $5,000 to $20,000. Again, you'll receive additional fees if you've been attached to the production entity. It is also possible to be paid a separate salary to write a treatment, even when you haven't been hired to write the TV screenplay. Since most TV movies have budgets in the ballpark of $2 million, as opposed to $20 million for an average feature budget, you can understand why television networks don't pay as much for ideas as do film studios.

If you sell the idea on which a sitcom is based, your big money will come from the royalties. It is imperative that you receive "Created by" credit; you might also go on staff as story editor, staff writer, or co-producer. A "Created by" credit will give you a royalty payment every week that the show airs and also a percentage on the back end . . . *à la* points in a movie. In features, you won't see points until the movie breaks into profit; in television, you won't get back-end money until the show is sold into syndication.

When you are debating how hard to push for the right to write the teleplay of your TV movie idea, remember that it's tougher to get hired as a first-time writer in television. In the fast-paced world of TV production and with their lower budgets, networks don't want to risk that the script you deliver won't be acceptable and that a new writer will have to be hired.

THE ART OF THE DEAL

Although we have used the consistent analogy of Hollywood as a game, I should stress that at this last stretch of the race the game-playing becomes quite serious. This is a time to be clear about what you want, about what is realistic and what is not. Once you've established your goals, let your agent or lawyer go in and play the game for you. These business-minded people will play in a businesslike fashion with their counterparts at the studio.

Bearing this general directive in mind, you can better yourself (through your negotiator's assistance) with some legitimate strategies that we'll now unveil:

Getting Paid to Walk Away

Yes, indeed. There are cases where it is to your advantage not to be hired as the first-draft writer. Frequently, you can parlay what may be a disappointment into quite a satisfactory opportunity on your next deal.

During one negotiation, a writing team was offered an additional $10,000 to what they were being offered for their idea in return for *not* negotiating to write the script. Of course, they wanted to write their project and earn a writing credit, but they received some advice from screenwriter and teacher Rick Pamplin that is worth noting: He told them to get their names attached to a story credit, get an agent, take the money for the idea, quit their day jobs, and spend their time writing a screenplay they really cared about—which could then also be sold.

Becoming a Part of the Production Entity

The methodology here can work in a couple of different ways. Let's suppose that you are a writer and not making a lot of money on your first deal. You can then propose to the studio that you want a bit more compensation on the back end of the current deal by becoming an associate producer. Translated, this says to the studio that they won't have to pay you that "little bit more compensation" unless the movie gets made. At the same time, you'll be obtaining better money and credit leverage for your next project. Most studios won't halt a deal over you demanding to be an associate producer. In broad terms, this is not a major credit but in some cases a beginner's credit. Undoubtedly, many individuals who are credited as associate producers are very talented people who contribute a great deal to various productions. Yet this slot is sometimes also available to the person who brought the story in or sold the idea to the studio.

If you are selling the idea without writing it and the story is well designed, you and your legal representative have an interesting negotiating opportunity. When you are dissatisfied with the money you're getting for the idea and disappointed that you're not getting hired to write it, your lawyer or agent can use this situation to your advantage. Your representative can propose to the studio this scenario: "Okay, you want to buy this idea, but you don't want to pay my client, Janet Smith, to write it. Since you are not giving her enough money on the story side, the only way to compensate her is to give her an associate producer credit and a salary if this movie gets made."

If you add these two fees together (story money and associate producer fee), then Janet Smith can possibly make more money than the amount she would have received for only the first-draft scriptwriting fee. By telling the studio that you wanted to write the script—*even if maybe you didn't*—your negotiator presents you as having made a sacrifice. That sacrifice is sometimes worth a credit and salary.

These strategies for acquiring credits will assist you in your attempts to make sure that your name winds up on the screen, since unfortunately you never know if you will land the on-film story credit. In your contract, of course, it can be stipulated that you created the story. But if four other writers come in after you, the credit must eventually be arbitrated at the Writers Guild. At that point your idea could have changed so much that you may not even receive story credit.

I might emphasize that the Writers Guild does lean heavily in favor of the first writer. In most cases, if the first writer has taken the precaution to register a story summary with the guild, that writer will receive—at the very least—a shared story credit. It is commonly felt that since the genesis of the movie is in that story summary, its creator deserves some credit. Furthermore, you may have a clause in your contract which specifies that if story credit is denied, you can receive a "Conceived by" or "Developed by" credit.

Before we move on to an overall philosophy of deal making, let me pause to underscore the point that each deal is important not only for what you receive, but also for what it can lead to in regard to your next deal. In fewer words, when making a deal, be future-minded. This isn't just one spin at the wheel. It's your career and there are times when career moves supersede money moves.

DEALS: MAKE THEM, DON'T BREAK THEM

Nobody wants to earn the reputation of being a lightweight, a wimp, or a fool. You won't be happy with a poorly negotiated contract. But don't be overly demanding at the early stages of your career and shut the door on later opportunities.

In the first laps of your Hollywood professional life, make the deals and respect the opportunity that you've received. Your foot is through the door and you can now continue to move ahead.

Back in my formative Hollywood years, my writing partner and I decided that the one thing we would never do is blow a deal. Our agents would call us up and tell us that the studio was taking advantage, that we were making a bad deal. Now we have slowly built up our careers and are in positions to get the better deals and to make stronger demands. Not blowing deals led to steady work and, ultimately, satisfying careers.

One of the best ways not to blow a deal is to realize that it is a joint venture. You and the studio have a mutual desire to make a movie. Understand that you are playing the game together.

Having returned once again to the Hollywood game metaphor, let's take an insider's view of the day-to-day participants as we scout for both the rewards and the penalties.

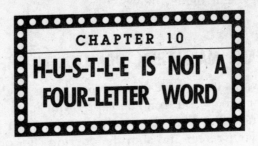

CHAPTER 10

H-U-S-T-L-E IS NOT A FOUR-LETTER WORD

"What's happening in Hollywood seems more like a lateral slide, a shuffling two-step danced to the music of the Hustle—quite literally, a coast, a dignified and stately approach to frenzy."

—*Maria Brenner in her book Going Hollywood*

So let's say you've just closed your first deal and a million things are going wrong. Maybe the script that gets handed in is a mess. Maybe it's wonderful but the studio doesn't think so. Maybe the studio loves it but the idea has been mistreated. Or maybe the movie was set to go and at the last minute was dropped from the production schedule. All of this and more can and will go wrong. Yet at the same time, other deals are being made right and left, while other motion pictures are being shot. What are you going to do? Despair or go back out there and do it again?

If you don't think you are cut out for hustling, or coasting, as described in the above quote, this is an opportunity to confront that reality. My advice is that you make a few contacts with various producers, or agents, and continue to develop good ideas. The fact that you've already sold one idea will encourage other people to listen more closely to your next pitches.

If you feel as though the gambling bug has bitten you, you may want to take a peek at the typical producer's day (yours truly) before you make your oath of commitment to Hollywood.

Like most other days on the planet, this Hollywood producer's day begins with . . .

Breakfast

The only difference is that mine is a breakfast meeting scheduled at eight in the morning at Hugo's in West Hollywood. What makes Hugo's a pleasant spot to meet is that it is filled with familiar faces from the industry; the feeling is reminiscent of the old studio commissary days.

On this morning, I am meeting with a writer who is pitching me ideas he hopes that I'll want to bring in to the studio where I'm currently based. After hearing two or three, one strikes me as exciting and I decide definitely to pitch it at my earliest opportunity. In the meantime, I promise to get back to the writer within a few weeks to let him know whether I'm having any luck with his idea.

Midmorning

After managing to return half of my calls, I wait for my ten o'clock appointment to arrive. For today's midmorning meeting, I'm going to be sitting down with Caitlin Buchman, president of motion picture development for Michael Landon Productions. I pitch her some of the more recent ideas I've been developing, hoping that one might make sense for her company. Depending on Michael's reaction too, I'll probably be hearing from her within the week. The meeting comes to an end in time for me to return a few more phone calls.

Late morning

I arrive at Columbia Studios, where I have a meeting with one of the vice presidents of development. Since he is a good friend, the meeting is very casual and he allows me to pitch four or five brief concepts. He promises to get back to me next week about whether or not we can develop any of the projects further, i.e. make a deal, and then begin to look for a writer.

Lunch

Here's an unusual meeting at the Columbia Bar & Grill in Hollywood. A journalist who works with the *Los Angeles Times* is curious as to how to go about selling some ideas as feature films or television movies. He feels that as a journalist he has unique access to true stories and wants to pitch some of those to me. I feel several of his ideas have potential, especially one television movie concept and we agree to meet next week to flesh out the story. I head back to my office for a few more phone calls.

Midafternoon

Next I meet a screenwriter who is already in the middle of a second draft. As a supervising producer on the project, my job is to meet with him and discuss any story problems he might be having. The meeting takes over two hours to complete, but I'm excited about the script's potential.

My executive assistant, Jeanine, informs me that there are no messages as I leave to go to Beverly Hills for my next stop.

Late Afternoon

At five o'clock I meet with one of the literary agents in the offices of CAA, and present some of the latest projects I have in the works. This agent covers the studio where I'm based and keeps tabs on what's being done there by meeting with the various producers. By finding out what we might have in development or going into development, she can match the various projects up with writers and stars that CAA represents.

Jeanine calls me at CAA with several messages, most of which I'm able to return. Then I'm on my way to a restaurant for a drinks meeting.

Early Evening

I meet with one of my producing partners for drinks and to talk about projects we might be able to work on together. We're both enthusiastic about one of the ideas and we agree to touch base again within the week.

Dinner

This meeting over dinner is with a writer I've recently met. We have a lengthy discussion about whether his story is commercial or not and finally agree to meet again next week.

And, of course, before the day is done, I make it home just in time for the eleven o'clock news. If I can, I try to read one script before falling asleep and then, no doubt, dream about some of the stories I'll be pitching at breakfast.

This was obviously only one version—a particularly jam-packed variation—of a producer's typical day. For other producers, writers, and idea people, other styles may apply. But ultimately it all boils down to getting the ball into play and not letting it drop. For that to happen, you have to hustle.

And before you decide that you're absolutely ready to give it your all, we will conclude our exploration with a look at some extremely useful protective gear that you can wear once you've set foot on the playing field.

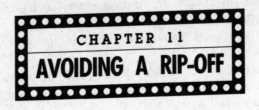

"Do unto others as you would have done unto you."
—The Golden Rule

As you become a player in the game, you will inevitably learn that not everyone in Hollywood plays fair. Sometimes there is retribution you can seek for having been exploited. Sometimes not. But rather than playing only defensively, opt to do so aggressively and intelligently. If you are constantly worried about getting ripped off, you won't sell anything because you'll never pitch. So let's focus on the intelligent safeguards first and foremost.

PROTECTING YOUR PROPERTY

Understand from the beginning that there is a difference between having the story of *E.T.* and just wanting to do a movie about extraterrestrials. The basic rule in legal protection is very clear: The broader the concept, the less protection you have. It would be impossible to claim a legal right to "a movie that takes place on an airplane" because this is far too broad an idea; this is part of the public domain. If your idea entails two specific characters arguing over a dead body they found on an airplane, then it would be much easier to claim a right to the story.

One essential device that protects your idea is also a prerequisite form of protection for the producer or studio executive. I'm referring to a standard release form, which both documents the submission of your idea and provides permission for the recipient to consider the idea. Any one-line idea submitted without a release will not be read in Hollywood. Period. So I suggest that with all your correspondence you use the standard release form that I have provided in the reference section at the back of this book. You may also want to make copies of it for multiple submissions. If a dispute arises, you can show that you followed the correct procedure in the submission of an idea by having enclosed the release. By the same token, producers and studios will not risk even looking at your idea before you have given them permission to do so. When submitting your idea with the release, be aware that the more specific you are about your topic, the more protection you will have. Make sure to include as many details in your outline as possible. Executives *will* be in touch with you if they like your idea. They *will* want to see more from you.

Technically, a one-liner cannot be copyrighted, nor can it be registered with the Writers Guild. Therefore, it's better to sit down and write a one- or two-page story synopsis (beginning, middle, and end) that clearly utilizes your concept, characters, and subject matter. This will supply you with something substantial enough to register.

Then call or write the west or east coast Writers Guild to request that they send you the envelopes which are used to store and seal written work. Once you get the envelope, write out an insert to be enclosed with your story synopsis that includes:

- The name of the project you are protecting
- The type of property—whether it is a motion picture or teleplay or series episode
- Your name and address

Then put this information and your story treatment into the envelope and seal it. When you mail this back to the Writers Guild, be sure to attach your check or money order on the *outside* of your sealed Writers Guild envelope, all enclosed within a larger mailing envelope. The fee is $10 for nonmembers on the West Coast, $15 for nonmembers on the East Coast. The sealed envelope will remain sealed unless there is a dispute over rights. Your material is protected this way for five years, at which time you must register it again. You are required to register all that you have written unbound on 8½-by-11-inch sheets of paper. This means no three-hole punch with brads and glossy folders. No stories written on paper bags or cocktail napkins. This is a legal document.

After you complete this process, you'll be sent a receipt from the Writers Guild that supplies you with your registration number for this project. Some people like to put their Writers Guild registration numbers on the title pages of their screenplays or outlines at all levels of submission. For handy reference in this regard, you can turn to the back of this book to find the phone number and address of both the east and west coast Writers Guild offices.

The guild, by the way, does not accept books, plays, music or lyrics, articles, photos, or drawings. Nor does it protect titles. In fact, you cannot copyright a title.

The alternate method of protecting material is to mail it in a self-addressed stamped envelope to yourself. If you do this frequently, however, I suggest that you make a notation or identification on the envelope so that you or someone else doesn't inadvertently open it. This approach will yield a legitimate, legal copyright for as long as the envelope remains sealed. For further information, you can contact the Copyright Office at the Library of Congress in Washington, D.C. That address has been listed for your convenience in our reference section as well.

We also spoke much earlier about your creating a secret

agenda with which to look for ideas. You may want to add to that agenda an item about secrecy. This shouldn't be an edict written in stone, but rather a warning against talking too much about your ideas when you are developing them. Some people have this weird habit of absorbing what they hear and truly not realizing that they've heard it from someone else.

I would be remiss not to tell you that the best protection is to write the screenplay based on your idea. As you can foresee, it would be much harder to steal your idea when it is tied into a fully realized script. When you have only that oneliner, the possibilities of it being stolen do increase. The guilty parties don't feel as guilty about taking it and justify themselves by rationalizing that it was only some little idea which they conveniently do not remember having heard from someone else.

Traveling on from this last statement, I'll bet you're wondering who those thieves might be. Let's see if we can help you identify them.

THE COMMON RIP-OFFS

The number one low-class acts who steal ideas are the people who advertise with the P.O. boxes in the various papers. Be a bit suspicious when these producers take you to lunch and tell you they love your script and ask you what other ideas you have. Be especially concerned when you have pitched them idea after idea but they never seem to get around to making an offer.

Beware of people who say they want to discuss a rewrite assignment but actually only want to hear your ideas about their latest script.

If you are a writer, another common scenario you may encounter is when a producer takes you to lunch with the overture that you're being considered as the writer to do a rewrite on a troublesome script. First, however, the producer would like your feedback on the latest draft of the script. Thinking that this is your shot at a writing job, you give very thorough feedback with some good ideas. Later, the producer will then thank you, but apologize in explaining that another writer was hired to do the rewrite. The next thing you know, the movie is released and dozens of your ideas are right up there on that screen.

In all honesty, I will admit that there is no foolproof way to protect an idea. If someone wants to rip off idea people like you and me, it can be done. It has been done. So you have to develop a form of inner radar as to who can be trusted. If you are going to be in the business of developing ideas, creating and pitching ideas, you must be prepared for the possibility of being ripped off. The less common rip-offs are usually termed "borrowing and changing" the ideas. These practices exist. Or, as they say—they come with the territory. If you're out there all over town pitching, presenting your ideas wherever or whenever you can, there is no absolute guarantee that someone unscrupulous won't nab an idea and modify it enough to clear his or her conscience and get the movie made. And you'll know in your heart that you were the one whose idea was the genesis of that movie. But you will have no way to prove it.

With that said, I've got some optimistic news about the following commodity:

INTEGRITY IN HOLLYWOOD

Most of the major studios and their executives, along with the major production companies, are wholly disinterested in stealing ideas. They do not stand to benefit by ripping people off. Why don't they? Because the way the game is structured in Hollywood, these entities profit by buying ideas legitimately. They would much rather option your ideas and pay you well for them than risk a lawsuit which would tie up the movie—much to everyone's misfortune. Nobody wants litigation; nobody wants lawsuits. Beyond that, recent precedents in cases that involved an idea person or writer versus the studio were judged in favor of the individual.

Most executives and producers at these legitimate companies believe, as I do, that you can make money and have integrity at the same time. When I am in the position of being pitched ideas or having them submitted to me, I must always operate with the awareness that to take someone else's idea and pitch it as my own would ruin my career. The minute word got out that I had stolen an idea, I would lose my livelihood. Not only would everyone stop submitting to me, but my reputation with the studios would be tarnished. I would not endanger my personal or my professional integrity. And I would wager that the greater percentage of working producers and studio executives live by the same philosophy.

During all my years in the role of pitching and selling ideas, there was only one incident I know of in which someone even came close to stealing an idea. Without my knowledge, a producer pitched my idea to the network. When I did find out, I informed this particular producer that I wanted the idea sold as a feature. The network ultimately made the TV movie (based on my idea) without paying anything to the producer or to me. However, the only one who lost was the producer. Six months down the road, I sold my story for a film, after all, and luckily nobody minded that there had been a TV movie dealing with the same subject.

If you see a movie made on a subject similar to yours, what has really been stolen? It doesn't mean that someone stole your story. And no one, as we've repeatedly observed, can own a subject. Should your subject be stolen, it must first be developed, written, replotted, and rewritten. With other people having done the work, how much did they really rip off from you? Should they steal your work—your story, your character, your plotting, and original premise—then you have a lawsuit which you definitely stand to win.

There are good ideas in the wind all the time. Different productions of very similar ideas are often in development simultaneously, even when the creative parties have had no contact. You simply can't sue someone for thinking like you. As one young writer said when she found out her idea was already in development, "At least I know I'm coming up with good ideas."

This brings us, by way of a rather circuitous route, back around to one of our original discoveries:

THE ENDURING POWER OF IDEAS

A good idea is worth protecting and worth detailing so that you make it your own special story. This will put you at an advantage in playing the game, in improving your financial and professional status. But it can do much more.

We have stressed all along that you should approach the movie business as a business. We have talked in depth about commercial and marketing strategies. By now, you surely know that Hollywood makes movies to make money, so it indeed looks for ideas that will continue to generate profit.

If your motivation to sell your idea to Hollywood is to make money, you can play the game and succeed. But if you have a deeper motivation to be a part of the magic that can be experienced in bringing a movie to life, you'll do much more than make some money. If you have ever been touched by that awe-inspiring magic of a movie—been moved, changed, exhilarated, or transported to another level of awareness—I'm sure you can imagine what it feels like to have had a hand in its unfolding. And if you would like to actually revel in the knowledge that your idea made it all happen, then you'll go the extra mile with your ideas—tend to them, say something a little different with them, give them story lines that express something that matters to you.

In my view, the miracle of movies can be traced back—through the twists and turns of all the technological and creative advancements and the countless individuals who've come together in this amazing collaborative process—to one thing: the idea. A brilliant idea to make pictures that move was what started everything. And ideas will continue to keep the whole ball rolling forward.

The heroes of Hollywood wear two hats each; they are both business people and creative people. They care about quality and, without being too presumptuous, I think that many care about the enduring contribution they are making to the art of the movies.

As a person with an idea to share, or a writer with a story to tell, or a producer who can present the idea to the powers that be, you can be the one who starts the ball rolling. In other words, when the movie finally gets made, only you—the person with the original idea—can honestly say you were there right from the very beginning. And that is what making it in Hollywood is all about.

CHAPTER 12
A HOLLYWOOD LAUNDRY LIST

And now that we have just about concluded on such a triumphant note, I take you back into the more rudimentary world where you need to have a practical approach. The following is a quick, convenient checklist to consult as to the marketability of your ideas before you submit them.

As you peruse these, I hope you find yourself pleasantly surprised at how much idea experience you've already gained.

. . . .

Does your idea leap off the page? Does it contain new inventions or a unique twist never seen on film before? Is your idea so creative and yet so obvious that you can't believe you or someone else didn't think of it before?

. . . .

If you have a mystery, are you sure that it isn't better suited to a one-hour television series?

. . . .

Action/adventure: Do you have your plot twist? Is your idea different enough from other movies in this genre and from those seen on television?

Can your idea be repeated? Is it simple? Could you hear people repeating the idea as if they have just heard a great joke?

If your idea is based on a tried-and-true concept, have you changed at least one ingredient? Have you changed a drama to a comedy or changed the sexes? Remember that Hollywood loves what has been successful in the past, if provided with a novel twist.

Is your hero sympathetic? Does the protagonist undergo a transformation?

Finally, here's a list of pitch pointers to help you succeed.

Never go in with only one idea. If that one doesn't ignite the listener, you'll have lost an opportunity and you may not have another chance.

Be sure that your ideas fall into different genres. Try for at least three areas—romantic comedy, thriller, and fantasy, for example.

Key words in delivery are: *articulate, brief, enthusiastic.*

Stress the central concept; remind the listener what the story is about.

. . . .

Pitch the concept—the one- or two-liners—before you get into the story. If you are prompted, briefly tell your story with its beginning, middle, and end. Touch the major plot points of Acts I, II, and III.

. . . .

If prompted even more, go into further detail as you allow the story and characters to come alive in the telling. But remember, pitching is concept, plot, story, subject—not characters and not dialogue.

. . . .

Stop the moment your listener appears to have lost interest. Ask if there are any questions or if you should go on to the next idea.

. . . .

The big Don'ts: Don't be desperate and don't be boring.

. . . .

The magic ingredient in a pitch is passion. It is contagious. When your love for your idea is evident, it helps sell your idea.

. . . .

Just before I bid each of you a fond farewell, I give you the option of continuing a step further. For the bold and daring, for those who think they are ready to sell to Hollywood—take a peek through one door that is already open to you.

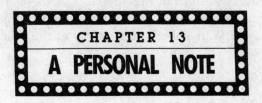

CHAPTER 13
A PERSONAL NOTE

And now for something completely different . . .

Sure, you've probably read lots of helpful "how to's" on Hollywood. Maybe you've attended some informative seminars or lectures about how to get into the business. Yet there is frequently a common complaint which arises: Now that you've got all these wonderful insights, what are you actually going to do with them?

Well, I hope what you do is roll up your sleeves and go to work. Get cracking on submissions of ideas—to agents, to the stars or directors, to the studios, to production companies, to producers like me, and, yes, to me.

There are two reasons I make this unusual proposal. First, I do so because I remember well how frustrating it was to have ideas but nowhere to go with them.

My second reason is a selfish one. My success, especially when juggling some dozens of projects in film and TV development—plus handling the ones that are getting made—is no longer dependent on me coming up with my own ideas but on finding and promoting other people's ideas.

Prior to me explaining how I work, I should stress that there are other equally competent producers who fulfill the same role that I do: We provide entry for those who have been locked out by the system.

I also want to emphasize that if you do decide to submit your ideas to me, do so by typing them on a three-by-five card or on standard stationery and make sure to enclose a completed release form (you will find samples A and B of the Standard Release form in the appendix of this book). If you do not include a release, I will not be able to consider your material. Mail your submissions to me at the following address:

· ·

Robert Kosberg
c/o IDEAS
P.O. Box 727
Hollywood, CA 90078

· ·

Please do not mail your ideas to the publisher of this book. HarperCollins will not be responsible in any way for ideas submitted to their offices. In receiving and reviewing your ideas, I am acting in my capacity as an independent producer and am in no way affiliated with HarperCollins Publishers, its parent company, or its affiliates. Furthermore, in considering your ideas, I am not acting in any of my current professional capacities in association with any agency, production company, studio, or their affiliates.

By completing and signing a standard release, you acknowledge that I am under no legal obligation to return the material or to respond to your submission and that neither I nor my employees can be held liable for the receipt of your ideas.

With these legal ramifications in mind, you can be assured that each and every idea properly submitted will be reviewed by a staff of capable people. While I absolutely can't promise that every submission will lead to a deal, I can guarantee that before your idea is pitched (if your idea is selected), you will first be contacted so that we can discuss our mutual roles in *your* deal. Never forget that you control the underlying rights to your idea, provided the idea is concrete, specific, and novel enough to enjoy protection under the law.

What the Middleman (or Middlewoman) Does

In essence, we "middlers" provide multi-access. We have established buyers throughout the industry to whom we have access and with whom we've made deals before. We can pitch an idea to the studios, the production companies, and to the agencies. We can perform the packaging role by taking ideas to the stars or to directors or writers who are looking for ideas.

As a Hollywood sort of matchmaker, I'm out there pitching every single day. When I'm back in my office, I'm listening to pitches from other writers or idea people.

How the Deal Is Approached

If, say, the studio likes your idea, they will want to deal first with your legal representative. Should you not have one, I can give you a list of names for you to use in finding an agent or lawyer that you like.

I cannot set my terms until yours are negotiated. Because you own the idea, until you are happy with your contract I can't proceed on the project. Once you're satisfied, then the studio comes to me, whereupon I request my producer's supervisory fee.

My reward comes only if the movie gets made. Then and only then will I get my producer's salary.

What I Look For

You may be surprised to learn that I don't necessarily go after only ideas that I like. Rather, I will select ideas that I think I can sell. So you needn't censor your submissions, even when you haven't fully developed the story, plot, or characters. If the idea appears to be marketable, I can often take part in fleshing out the idea.

Do let me know, by way of an enclosure, whether you

desire to write the screenplay and whether or not you have a writing sample.

"Middlers" versus Agents

Producers who serve in my capacity are not agents. We don't function as agents and we don't take ten percent of your salary. Neither do I perform the agent's task of developing your overall career. I am more than happy to work in conjunction with your agent, as long as our submissions aren't in conflict.

To those of you who haven't been able to get an agent, producers such as myself offer a unique "in" to the business at a somewhat advanced point of entry for someone who would otherwise be forced to pound the pavement.

When Submitted Ideas Are Similar

My protocol with similar submissions is to choose in favor of the earliest postmark. This is especially the case when different people clip the same article to enclose as an idea based on a true story.

When I find a good idea and partner with its creator, I can tell you that I am driven to get it sold. I have an investment: If this movie gets made I will be its producer—I will continue to earn my livelihood. I've been known to pitch an idea for years, if that's what it takes. Good ideas aren't easy to find, but once they're found, I consistently attempt to get them produced.

I never give up. If I can't sell it one way, I'll try another approach. I'll take it to a star, change it into a TV movie— whatever it takes. I suppose you could say that I like the challenge.

So now the challenge has fallen to you. Wherever you submit or pitch your future movies, let me just say—may the best ideas win!

APPENDIX: REFERENCE MATERIALS

RESEARCH SOURCES

Adams, Cecil. *The Straight Dope: Answers to Questions That Torment Everyone.* Ballantine Books.

———. *More of Straight Dope.* Ballantine Books.

Alden, Todd. *Finding Facts Fast.* Ten Speed Press.

Ashe, Arthur, Jr. *A Hard Road to Glory: A History of the African American Athletes Since 1946.* Warner Books.

Barzini, Luigi. *The Italians: A Full-Length Portrait Featuring Their Manners and Morals.* Atheneum.

Berlitz, Charles. *Charles Berlitz's World of Strange Phenomena.* Wynwood.

Bonds, Ray, ed. *The Illustrated Dictionary of Modern American Weapons.* Prentice-Hall.

Brookesmith, Peter. *Appearances and Disappearances: Strange Comings and Goings from the Bermuda Triangle.* Chartwell Books.

———. *The UFO Casebook.* Chartwell Books.

Byrne, Robert. *The 637 Best Things Anybody Ever Said.* Fawcett Books.

Canning, John. *50 Strange Stories of the Supernatural.* Bonanza.

Ciardi, John. *A Browser's Dictionary: A Compendium of Curious Expressions and Intriguing Facts.* Harper & Row.

Corbeil, Jean Claude. *The Facts-on-File Visual Dictionary.* Facts-on-File.

Cousteau, Jacques. *The Ocean World.* Harry Abrams.

Curtis, Natalie, ed. *The Indians' Book of Authentic Native American Legends, Lore and Music.* Bonanza.

Dunan, Marcel, ed. *Larousse Encyclopedia of Modern History from 1500 to the Present Day*. Crescent.

Feldman, David. *Imponderables: The Solution to the Mysteries of Everyday Life*. Quill.

———. *Why Do Clocks Run Clockwise and Other Imponderables*. Perennial Library.

Funk, Charles Earle. *Hog on Ice: The Origin and Development of the Pungent and Colorful Phrases We All Use*. Harper & Row.

Goldberg, M. Hirsch. *The Blunder Book: Colossal Errors, Minor Mistakes and Surprising Slipups That Have Changed the Course of History*. Quill.

Habenstein, Robert, and William Lamers. *Funeral Customs the World Over*. Bulfin Printers.

Henry, Lewis C., ed. *Best Quotations for All Occasions*. Fawcett Books.

Hirsch, Edward, Jr., Joseph Fikett, and James Trefil. *The Dictionary of Cultural Literacy: What Every American Needs to Know*. Houghton Mifflin.

Israel, Betsy. *Grown-up Fast: A True Story of Teenage Life in Suburban America*. Poseiden Press.

Johnson, June. *838 Ways to Amuse a Child*. Gramercy.

Jones, Judy and William Wilson. *An Incomplete Education*. Ballantine Books.

Kidron, Michael, and Ronald Segal. *The New State of the World Atlas*. Touchstone.

Kinder & Higerman. *The Anchor Atlas of World History*. Doubleday.

Kisselhoff, Jeff. *You Must Remember This: An Oral History of Man from the 1890s to World War II*. Harcourt Brace Jovanovich.

Langer, William L., ed. *The Encyclopedia of World History*. Doubleday.

Macaulay, David. *The Way Things Work*. Houghton Mifflin.

Maltby, Richard. *Passing Parade: A History of Popular Culture in the 20th Century*. Oxford University Press.

Marlin, John Tepper. *Cities of Opportunity: A Comprehensive Guide to Finding the Best Place to Work, Live and Prosper in the 1990s and Beyond*. Master Media.

Miller, Laurence M. *Barbarians to Bureaucrats: Corporate Life Cycle Strategies and Lessons From the Rise and Fall of Civilization*. Clarkson Potter.

Moyers, Bill. *A World of Ideas*. Doubleday.

Nash, Jay Robert. *Jay Robert Nash's Crime Chronology: A World-Wide Record 1900–1983*. Facts-on-File.

Poundstone, William. *Big Secrets: The Uncensored Truth About All Sorts of Stuff You Are Never Supposed to Know*. Quill.

Tuleja, Tad. *Curious Customs: The Stories Behind 296 Popular American Rituals*. Harmony Books.

Vare, Ethlie Ann, and Greg Ptacek. *Mothers of Invention: From the Bra to the Forgotten Women and Their Unforgettable Ideas*. William Morrow.

STANDARD REFERENCE BOOKS

American Men and Women of Science
Baker's Biographical Dictionary of Musicians
Barron's Student's Concise Encyclopedia
Bartlett's Familiar Quotations
Benet's Readers Encyclopedia
Biographical Index
Britannica Book of Popular Science
Chambers' World Gazetteer
Chronicle of the 20th Century
Columbia Lippincott Gazetteer of the World
The Complete Film Dictionary
Current Biography
B. Dalton's World Almanac & Book of Facts
Dictionary of American Biography
A Dictionary of Americanisms on Historical Principle
A Dictionary of Slang and Unconventional English
Encyclopedia of American Crime
Encyclopedia Americana
Encyclopedia Britannica
The Filmgoer's Companion
Fishbein's Medical and Health Encyclopedia
Grzimek's Animal Life Encyclopedia
Halliwell's Film and Video Guide
Information Please Almanac

International Motion Picture Almanac
International Wildlife Encyclopedia
March's Thesaurus Dictionary
McGill's Survey of Cinema
McGraw-Hill Dictionary of Art
McGraw-Hill Encyclopedia of World Art
Official Encyclopedia of Sports and Games
Oxford Companion to Film
Oxford Encyclopedia
People, Places and Things: A Volume of Ideas, Living, Dying, Dead, and Fossil, Which We Are Moved By or Were Moved By
People's Almanac
Reader's Digest Stories Behind Everyday Things
Reader's Guide to Periodical Literature
The Trivia Encyclopedia
Webster's Biographical Dictionary
Who's Who
World Book Encyclopedia

STARS WITH PRODUCTION COMPANIES

At the time this book went to press, several of the addresses I had provided had already changed. So, in addition to advising you to use the list with discretion and not be overly aggressive in writing to these companies, I would suggest that you doublecheck with the studio you want to contact to see if a forwarding address exists. Please restrict your communication to writing; placing unsolicited phone calls to these companies is a particularly unproductive practice.

Chevy Chase
Cornelius Productions
2916 Main Street #200
Santa Monica, CA 90405

Cher
Isis Productions
c/o Columbia Pictures
Columbia Plaza
Burbank, CA 91505

Robert De Niro
Tribeca Productions
166 Franklin Street
New York, NY 10013

Griffin Dunne
Double Play Productions
1250 Broadway/33rd fl.
New York, NY 10001

Clint Eastwood
Malpaso Productions
c/o Warner Bros. Pictures
4000 Warner Blvd.
Burbank, CA 91522

Sally Field
Fogwood Films
c/o Columbia Pictures
Columbia Plaza
Burbank, CA 91505

Jane Fonda
Fonda Films
P.O. Box 491355
Los Angeles, CA 90049

Michael J. Fox
Snowback Productions
c/o Paramount Pictures
5555 Melrose Avenue
Los Angeles, CA 90038

Tom Hanks
c/o Walt Disney Pictures
500 S. Buena Vista Street
Burbank, CA 91521

Mark Harmon
Wings Productions, Inc.
c/o Paramount Pictures
5555 Melrose Avenue
Los Angeles, CA 90038

Goldie Hawn
Hawn-Sylbert Movie Co.
c/o Hollywood Pictures
500 S. Buena Vista Street
Animation Bldg. 1D6
Burbank, CA 91521

Pee-wee Herman
c/o Paramount Pictures
5555 Melrose Avenue
Los Angeles, CA 90038

Jessica Lange
Prairie Films
c/o Universal Pictures
100 Universal City Plaza
  Bungalow 72
Universal City, CA 91608

Shelley Long
Itsbinso Long, Inc.
c/o Walt Disney Pictures
500 S. Buena Vista Street
Burbank, CA 91521

Madonna
Siren Films
c/o Columbia Pictures
Columbia Plaza
Burbank, CA 91505

Bette Midler
All Girl Productions
c/o Walt Disney Pictures
500 S. Buena Vista Street
Burbank, CA 91521

Eddie Murphy
Eddie Murphy Productions
c/o Paramount Pictures
5555 Melrose Avenue
Los Angeles, CA 90038

Bronson Pinchot
c/o Lorimar
10202 W. Washington Blvd.
Culver City, CA 90232

Victoria Principal
Principal Productions
310 N. San Vicente Blvd. #207
Los Angeles, CA 90048

Richard Pryor
c/o Columbia Pictures
Columbia Plaza
Burbank, CA 91505

Dennis Quaid
Summers-Quaid Productions
c/o Orion Pictures
1888 Century Park East/6th fl.
Los Angeles, CA 90067

Robert Redford
Wildwood Enterprises, Inc.
1101 Montana Avenue #E
Santa Monica, CA 90403

Molly Ringwald
Kelbath Productions
c/o Columbia Pictures
Columbia Plaza/Bungalow #2B
Burbank, CA 91522

Tom Selleck
c/o Hollywood Pictures
500 S. Buena Vista Street
Burbank, CA 91505

Martin Sheen
Symphony Pictures
5711 W. Slauson Blvd. #226
Culver City, CA 90230

Bruce Willis
Hudson Hawk Films
c/o Tri-Star Pictures
1875 Century Park East
Los Angeles, CA 90067

Henry Winkler
Monument Pictures
Paramount Pictures
5555 Melrose Avenue
Los Angeles, CA 90038

DIRECTORS WITH PRODUCTION COMPANIES

Jim Abrahams
c/o Walt Disney Pictures
500 S. Buena Vista Street
Burbank, CA 91521

David Anspaugh
c/o Orion Pictures
1888 Century Park East
Los Angeles, CA 90067

John Badham
Badham-Cohen Group
100 Universal City
Plaza/Bldg. 127
Universal City, CA 91608

Martin Bregman
Bregman Productions
c/o Universal Pictures
100 Universal City Plaza
Universal City, CA 91608

Martin Brest
City Lights Films
c/o Universal Pictures
100 Universal City Plaza
    Bungalow 424
Universal City, CA 91608

Mel Brooks
Brooksfilm, Ltd.
c/o Twentieth Century Fox
    Film Corp.
10201 West Pico Blvd.
Los Angeles, CA 90035

James Cameron
Tech Noir Productions
270 N. Canon Drive #1195
Beverly Hills, CA 90210

Wes Craven
Craven Films
8271 Melrose Avenue
Los Angeles, CA 90046

Joe Dante
Renfield Productions
c/o Warner Bros. Pictures
4000 Warner Blvd./Bldg. 103 #1
Burbank, CA 91522

George Roy Hill
Pan Arts Productions
c/o Warner Bros. Pictures
4000 Warner Blvd.
Burbank, CA 91522

Walter Hill
The Phoenix Company
c/o Carolco
8800 Sunset Blvd.
Los Angeles, CA 90069

Arthur Hiller
c/o Tri-Star Pictures
1875 Century Park East
Los Angeles, CA 90067

John Hughes
Hughes Entertainment
c/o Universal Pictures
100 Universal City Plaza
Universal City, CA 91608

Peter Hyams
Peter Hyams Inc.
c/o Paramount Pictures
5555 Melrose Avenue
Los Angeles, 90038

Henry Jaglom
International Rainbow Pictures
9165 Sunset Blvd./Penthouse
 300
Los Angeles, CA 90069

Roland Joffe
Lightmotive Ltd.
c/o Warner Bros. Pictures
4000 Warner Blvd.
Burbank, CA 91522

Randal Kleiser
Randal Kleiser Productions
2400 Broadway #100
Santa Monica, CA 90404

Jim Kouf
Kouf-Bigelow Productions
c/o Walt Disney Pictures
400 S. Buena Vista Street
Burbank, CA 91521

Barry Levinson
c/o Tri-Star Pictures
1875 Century Park East
Los Angeles, CA 90067

Penny Marshall
c/o Twentieth Century Fox
 Film Corp.
10201 West Pico Blvd.
Los Angeles, CA 90035

Nicholas Meyer
Pari Passu Productions
c/o Paramount Pictures
5555 Melrose Avenue
Los Angeles, CA 90038

James D. Parriott
James D. Parriott Productions
c/o New World Entertainment
1440 S. Sepulveda Blvd.
Los Angeles, CA 90025

Daniel Petrie
Daniel Petrie Productions
13201 Haney Place
Los Angeles, CA 90049

Ivan Reitman
Ivan Reitman Productions
c/o The Burbank Studios
4000 Warner Blvd.
Burbank, CA 91522

Herb Ross
c/o Tri-Star Pictures
1875 Century Park East
Los Angeles, CA 90067

Tony Scott
Slow Scan Productions
c/o Columbia Pictures
Columbia Plaza West #1
Burbank, CA 91505

Andrew Solt
The Solt-Egan Company
9121 Sunset Blvd.
Los Angeles, CA 90069

Steven Spielberg
Amblin Entertainment
100 Universal City Plaza
  Bungalow 477
Universal City, CA 91608

Martin Starger
Marstar Productions
c/o Twentieth Century Fox
  Film Corp.
10201 West Pico Blvd.
Los Angeles, CA 90035

David Zucker
Zucker Brothers Productions
11777 San Vicente Blvd. #640
Los Angeles, CA 90049

RANGE OF MONIES FOR WRITERS' WORK

The Writers Guild publishes a booklet called the *Schedule of Minimums*, which can be bought for $1. This booklet states the minimum payment writers can expect for their work. The following chart contains "flat deal" figures applicable to writers who have not previously been employed in television, theatrical films, or radio.

The rates are divided into a low end and a high end, depending on the cost of the entire production budget. A low budget is considered less than $2.5 million. A high budget is $2.5 million or more. In the following chart, the first figure given, both low and high, is for the period beginning September 1, 1989, through February 28, 1991. The second period is effective from March 1, 1991, through May 1, 1992.

EMPLOYMENT, FLAT DEALS, SCREENPLAY

| | 9/1/89–2/28/91 | | 3/1/91–5/1/92 | |
	Low	High	Low	High
Screenplay, including treatment:	$28,245	$52,524	$29,516	$54,888
Installments— delivery of treatment:	10,590	16,144	11,067	16,870
Delivery of first-draft screenplay:	12,709	24,216	13,281	25,306
Delivery of final-draft screenplay:	4,944	12,164	5,166	12,711

EMPLOYMENT, FLAT DEALS, SCREENPLAY (*CONTINUED*)

| | 9/1/89–2/28/91 | | 3/1/91–5/1/92 | |
	Low	High	Low	High
Screenplay, excluding treatment:	17,650	36,321	18,444	37,955
Installments— delivery of first-draft screenplay:	12,709	24,216	13,281	25,306
Delivery of final-draft screenplay:	4,941	12,104	5,163	12,649
Additional compensation for story included in screenplay:	4,038	12,104	4,220	8,434
Story or treatment:	10,590	16,144	11,067	16,870
Original treatment:	14,624	24,216	15,282	25,306

FIRST-DRAFT SCREENPLAY, WITH OR WITHOUT OPTION FOR FINAL-DRAFT SCREENPLAY:

| | 9/1/89–2/28/91 | | 3/1/91–5/1/92 | |
	Low	High	Low	High
First-draft screenplay:	$12,709	$24,216	$13,281	$25,306
Final-draft screenplay:	8,471	16,144	8,852	16,870
Rewrite of screenplay:	10,590	16,144	11,067	16,870
Polish of screenplay:	5,297	6,071	5,535	8,434

TELEVISION NETWORK PRIME TIME—30 MINUTES

	9/1/89–2/28/91	3/1/91–5/1/92
Story:	$ 4,261	$ 4,453
Teleplay installments:		
First draft:	9,170	9,583

Final compensation: 60% of agreed compensation but not less than 90% of minimum balance of agreed compensation.

| Story and teleplay: | 12,785 | 13,360 |

Story and teleplay installments:

Story: 30% of agreed compensation

First-draft teleplay: 40% of agreed compensation or the difference between the story installment and 90% of minimum, whichever is greater.

Final-draft teleplay: Balance of agreed compensation.

On story pilots, the writer is to be paid 10% of the first installment (as an advance against such first installment) upon commencement of services. The applicable minimum for a pilot story or story and teleplay is 150% of the applicable minimum set forth above.

NETWORK PRIME TIME—60 MINUTES

	9/1/89–2/28/91	3/1/91–5/1/92
Story:	$ 7,501	$ 7,839
Teleplay:	12,369	12,926
Story and teleplay:	18,801	19,647

Story and teleplay installments:

Story: 30% of agreed compensation.

First-draft teleplay: 40% of agreed compensation or the difference between the story installment and 90% of minimum, whichever is greater.

Final-draft teleplay: Balance of agreed compensation.

On story pilots, the writer is to be paid 10% of the first installment (as an advance against such first installment) upon commencement of services. The applicable minimum for a pilot story or story and teleplay is 150% of the applicable minimum set forth above.

NETWORK PRIME TIME—120 MINUTES, NONEPISODIC

	9/1/89–2/28/91	3/1/91–5/1/92
Story:	$14,608	$15,265
Teleplay:	24,954	26,077

First draft: 60% of agreed compensation but not less than 90% of minimum.

Final draft: Balance of agreed compensation.

Story and teleplay: 38,043   39,755

Story and teleplay installments:

Story: 30% of agreed compensation.

First-draft teleplay: 40% of agreed compensation or the difference between the story installment and 90% of minimum, whichever is greater.

Final-draft teleplay: Balance of agreed compensation.

NETWORK PRIME-TIME RERUNS

As to stories and/or teleplays, compensation for all reruns on a network in prime time is payable at 100% of applicable minimums. However, the applicable minimum for the purpose of calculating all rerun compensation is the minimum applicable to "other than network prime time" television films.

The minimum compensation payable with respect to other reruns in the United States and Canada other than on a network in prime time is as follows:

2nd Run: 50% of applicable minimum if on a network; otherwise, 40%.

3rd Run: 40% of applicable minimum if on a network; otherwise, 30%.

4th, 5th, and
6th Run: 25% of applicable minimum for *each* such run.

7th, 8th, 9th, and
10th Run: 15% of applicable minimum for *each* such run.

11th and 12th Run: 10% of applicable minimum for *each* such run.

13th Run and *each* run
thereafter: 5% of applicable minimum for *each* such run.

THE WRITERS GUILD

The Writers Guild of America East serves writers living east of the Mississippi; Writers Guild of America West serves those west of the Mississippi. For registering scripts or obtaining general information, use the address or phone number corresponding to your part of the country.

Writers Guild of America East
555 West 57th Street
New York, NY 10010
212-245-6180

Writers Guild of America West
8955 Beverly Boulevard
West Hollywood, CA 90048
213-550-1000

COPYRIGHT INFORMATION

You can request copyright information at the following address:

Copyright Office
Library of Congress
Washington, DC 20559

STANDARD RELEASE FORMS

The following two sample standard release forms are legal agreements. Read them carefully if you are going to use them for submitting your ideas to me or to any legitimate entertainment industry entity. Remember that no person can legally look at your submission without an accompanying release. In going over the terms that are spelled out, you should note that they exist to protect your idea from being used without your consent. The terms also protect the recipient from any obligation to use your idea and from any legal recourse or action you might take regarding the use of the idea if your consent has been given.

Standard Release A

As of _____ , 19___

_____
_____
_____
_____

Ladies and Gentlemen:

I submit herewith to you certain written material ("Material") described for identification purposes as:

_____.

I acknowledge that the Material was created and written by me without any suggestion or request from you that I write or create the Material. I am executing and submitting this letter in consideration of your agreement to review the Material with the express understanding that I limit and subject my claim of rights as follows:

You will not use the Material or any part thereof unless either: (a) you shall hereafter enter into a written agreement with the lawful owner of the Material or the owner of the rights involved with respect to the use thereof; in no event shall any such agreement be implied, and that no obligation of any kind on your part to me or any other person, firm or corporation is assumed by you, or may be implied against you, in connection with the submission of the Material in the absence of a written agreement; or (b) you shall determine in good faith that you have the independent legal right to use all or any part of (or any features or elements in) the Material without my consent, either because such material so used is not new or novel, or is in the public domain, or otherwise not legally protected or protectable, or was not fixed in a tangible means of expression or was obtained by you from other sources, including your own employees.

Should you proceed under (b) above, and should I dispute your right to do so, I undertake the entire burden of proof of originality, access, copying and all other elements necessary to establish your liability, and agree that my submission of the Material shall in no event give rise to a presumption or inference of copying or taking, or to a presumption or inference that anyone in your organization, other than the particular individual to whom the Material is delivered by me, had access to the Material or examined the same; and I further agree that, should I bring any action against you for wrongful appropriation of the Material or any part thereof, such action shall be limited to an action at law for damages (which shall in no event, under any theory, exceed the fair market value of the Material on the date hereof, as determined by customary practice in the motion picture industry); that I shall in no event be entitled to an injunction or any other equitable relief; and that, should I be unsuccessful in any such action, I assume, and agree to pay to you upon demand, all of your costs and expenses entailed in defending or contesting such action, including all court costs, costs of depositions, attorneys' fees, and the fees or charges of any experts engaged by you to ascertain originality, public domain status, or any other facts or factors deemed necessary or advisable by you in the defense or contest of such action. I further agree that, as a condition precedent to any such action, I will give you written notice of my contention that you have no right to proceed under (b) above, stating the particulars in complete detail; and that any such action shall be, and is hereby forever waived and barred, unless duly filed by me within six (6) months after your first public release or use of the Material, or thirty (30) days after you notify me in writing that you deny liability to me, whichever is earlier.

In agreeing to the provisions of the preceding paragraph, I understand that I may be waiving rights with respect to claims that are at this time unknown or unsuspected, and in accordance with such waiver, I hereby acknowledge that I have read and understand, and hereby expressly waive the benefits of Section 1542 of the Civil Code of California, which provides as follows:

> "A general release does not extend to claims which the creditor does not know or suspect to exist in his favor at the time of executing the release, which if known by him must have materially affected his settlement with the debtor."

I have retained a copy of the Material and agree that you shall not be obligated to return the Material to me unless and until you receive my written request therefor, and I release you from all liability if the Material is lost, misplaced, stolen or destroyed.

I hereby acknowledge you are under no obligation to use the Material in any manner.

I further represent and warrant that I am the author and sole and exclusive owner of the Material and of all rights in and to the Material, and that I have full power and authority to submit the Material to you on the aforesaid terms and conditions, each and all of which shall be binding on me, and on my agents, heirs and assigns. This Agreement shall inure to your benefit and to the benefit of your parent, subsidiary and affiliated corporations and each of their officers, employees and agents.

Very truly yours,

_____

(Signature)

_____

Name (print)

_____

Address

_____

City/State/Zip

_____

Telephone

ACCEPTED:

By: _____

cc:

Standard Release A

As of _____ , 19___

Proposed title (if any) of material submitted:

_____.
_____
_____
_____
_____

Ladies and Gentlemen:

I am on this date submitting for possible use by you my material identified herein (hereinafter called the "Material") in accordance with the understanding, and subject to the conditions, set forth herein. I acknowledge that the Material was created and written by me without any suggestion or request from you that I write or create the Material. I have attached hereto a copy of said Material, a synopsis thereof, or a complete description of such Material if in film or tape form. I am executing and submitting this letter in consideration of your agreement to review the material with the express understanding that I limit my claim of rights to the features of the Material as specifically synopsized or as attached hereto.

1. Except as otherwise specifically stated herein, I represent:
   a. That the Material is original with me;

   b. That I have the exclusive right to grant all rights in the Material; and

   c. I have exclusive rights in the title, if any, with regard to its use in connection with the Material.

2. You agree that you will not use the Material unless you shall first negotiate with me compensation for such use, but I under-

stand and agree that your use of material containing features and elements similar to or identical with those contained in the Material shall not obligate you to negotiate with me nor entitle me to any compensation if you determine that you have an independent legal right to use such other material which is not derived from me (either because such features and elements were not new or novel, or were not originated by me, or because other persons [including your employees] have submitted or may hereafter submit material containing similar or identical features or elements which you have the right to use).

3. I agree that I must give you written notice by certified or registered mail at your address as set forth in the address portion of this letter, of any claim arising in connection with said Material or arising in connection with this agreement, within the period of time prescribed by the applicable statute of limitations, but in no event more than ninety (90) calendar days after I acquire knowledge of facts sufficient to put me on notice of any such claim, as an express condition precedent to the initiation of legal action hereunder. My failure to so give you written notice will be deemed an irrevocable waiver of any rights I might otherwise have with respect to such claim. I shall further withhold filing any legal action for a period of thirty (30) days after said written notice to allow you time to investigate any claim.

4. I have retained a copy of said Material, and I release you from any liability for loss or other damage to the copy or copies submitted by me.

5. I hereby state that I have read and understand this agreement; that no oral representations of any kind have been made to me; that there are no prior or contemporaneous oral agreements in effect between us pertaining to said Material; and that this agreement states our entire understanding. Any provision or part of any provision which is void or unenforceable shall be deemed omitted, and this agreement with such provision or part thereof